DATE DUE

DEC 08 1992			

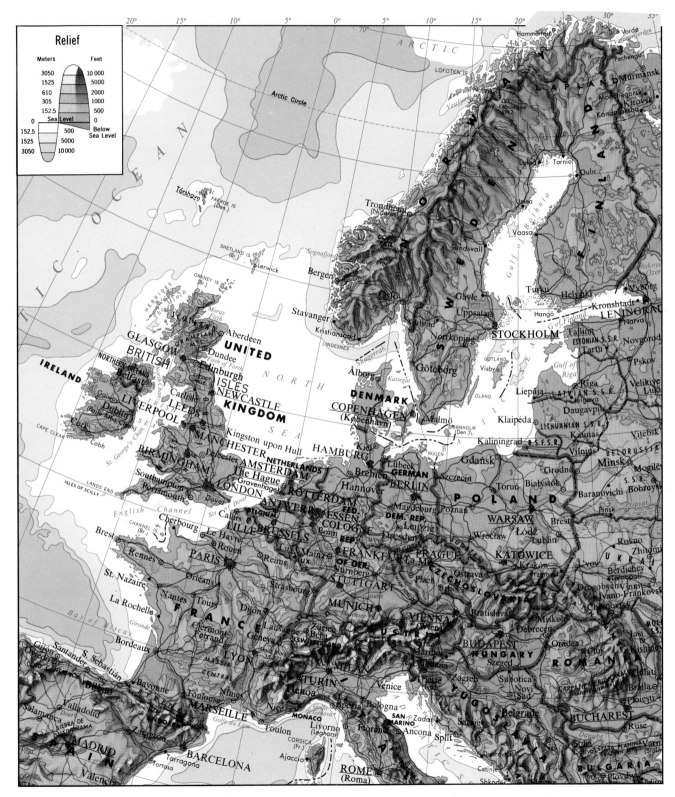

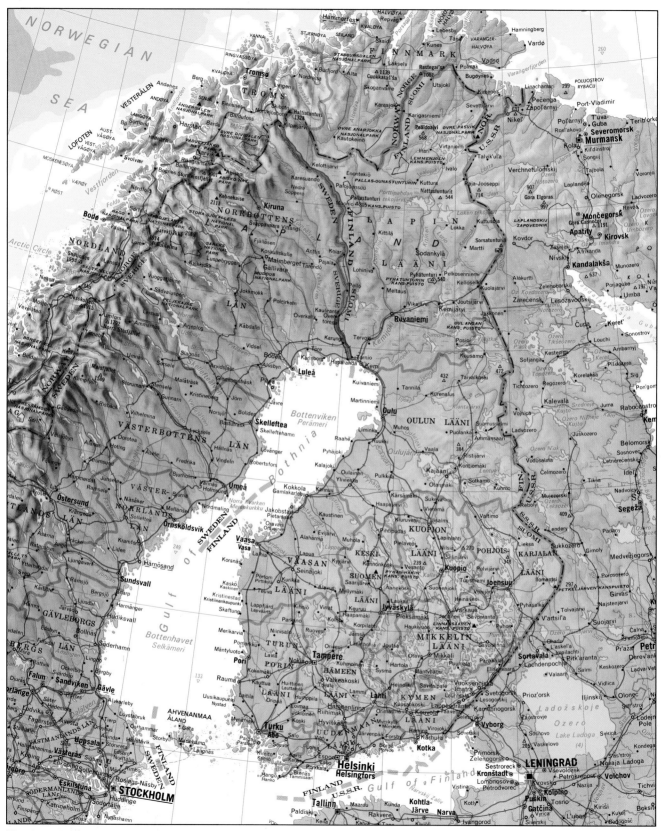

Enchantment of the World

FINLAND

By Martin Hintz

Consultant: Professor Börje Vähämäki, Lic. Fil., Department of Scandinavian, University of Minnesota, Minneapolis, Minnesota

Consultant for Social Studies: Donald W. Nylin, Ph.D., Assistant Superintendent for Instruction, Aurora West Public Schools, Aurora, Illinois

Consultant for Reading: Robert L. Hillerich, Ph.D., Bowling Green State University, Bowling Green, Ohio

CP CHILDRENS PRESS, CHICAGO

The city of Naantali

For the Finns of the Winter War, who showed what courage means.

For help in preparing this book, the author would like to thank the Finnish Ministry for Foreign Affairs and its Press and Cultural Center; the economic department of the Ministry of Finance; the Agricultural Information Center of Finland; Finnair airlines; my good friends Patricof and Nino de Prado of the Finland National Tourist Office; the Embassy of Finland; the staff and administration of Suomi University in Hancock, Michigan; Press Consul Ritva-Liisa Elomaa of the Consulate General of Finland; and the editors of *The Scandinavian Review*. Special appreciation must be offered to Kaj Grundstrom, Sara Ekelund, Jouni Mykkanen, Kaija Boos, Irmeli Torssonen, Captain Kari Aarnio, Mrs. Satu Tiivola, Pekka and Ann Marie Sahenkari, and the many other wonderful Finns who, by sharing themselves, showed how wonderful Finland really is.

Library of Congress Cataloging in Publication Data

Hintz, Martin
  Finland.

  (Enchantment of the world)
  Includes index.
  Summary: Explores the geography, history, traditions, social life, and arts of the country which sits astride the Arctic Circle.
  1. Finland—Juvenile literature. [1. Finland]
I. Title. II. Series.
DL1012.H53 1983   948.91   82-17856
ISBN 0-516-02764-6   AACR2

Picture Acknowledgments

Finland National Tourist Office: Pages 4, 9, 11 (top), 14, 17, 18, 20, 21, 26, 28, 32, 43, 47, 48, 50 (bottom), 51 (bottom), 53, 54, 56, 59, 60, 61, 62, 64, 71, 74, 75, 76, 77, 79, 80 (bottom), 84, 87, 88, 90, 92, 96, 97, 98, 99, 101, 102, 103, 104, 105 (right), 106, 107, 108, 109, 114, 123
Colour Library International: Cover, pages 5, 6, 24, 46, 50 (top), 51 (top), 66, 69, 72, 80 (top), 105 (left)
Jerry Hennen: Page 8
Martin Hintz: Pages 11 (bottom), 12, 13, 23, 36, 39, 55, 63, 65, 78, 83, 120
Historical Pictures Service, Inc., Chicago: Pages 34, 35
Wide World Photos: Page 44
Chandler Forman: Page 51
Len Meents: Maps on pages 50, 59, 60, 61
Courtesy Flag Research Center, Winchester, Massachusetts 01890: Flag on back cover
Cover: South Harbor Market, Helsinki

A dense forest is reflected in the calm water of one of Finland's thousands of lakes.

TABLE OF CONTENTS

Porvoo, founded in 1346, is known as the city of poets and painters.

Chapter 1

LAND OF
THE UNEXPECTED

Bellowing and roaring, the huge moose thundered across the highway and disappeared into the dense pine woods on the far side of a ditch. Cars and buses skidded to a halt. Their tires screeched in protest as the creature stampeded past. One Volkswagen, bumped from behind by another vehicle, almost slid into a ditch. Only fast wheel-and-brake action prevented a collision.

It's not every day that a motorist in Finland comes so close to being run over by a charging bull moose.

"Did you see those glaring red eyes?" "Wow, the size of that thing!" "Those antlers must have been a mile wide!" Everyone who stopped at the side of the road was talking at once. But as quickly as it came, the animal was gone, lost in the dark Finnish forest midway between Helsinki and Porvoo.

"You know," said a guide from one of the tour buses stopped in the traffic jam, "that's really an elk, not a moose." A debate immediately started about what moose and elk actually look like. But it ended on a laughing note. After all, the North American

In North America, this animal is called a moose, in Finland an elk.

moose is the same animal as the European elk, the creature that had just dashed by. The two are separated only by thousands of miles—and a migration that took place a few thousand years ago. So the Finns call the animal an elk; the Americans call it a moose—some difference!

Finland is full of such surprises. It's a forested land, dark and deep, where one can almost see the woodland spirits from the Finnish epic tale, the *Kalevala*.

Finland is astride the Arctic Circle, hanging midway between summer and winter all year round. It is a long, narrow country, tucked between Sweden, Norway, and the Soviet Union. It has added traditions from these countries to a very special Finnish foundation.

*Finland has become a vacation retreat for thousands of
visitors each year. Many of them visit the Åland Islands (above).*

Because of their strategic location, the Finns have been
trampled, colonized, massacred, and fought over for hundreds of
years. The Swedes ruled the land for generations; then Finland
became an autonomous part of the tsar's Russia. The Germans
occupied northern Finland (Lapland) during World War II. But
they never ruled Finland and were chased out at the end of the
war. All that passing back and forth of governments would be
enough to exhaust any people. But the Finns are now holding
their own and getting sweet "revenge" on their former
conquerors. Today, Swedes, Russians, and Germans all travel to
Finland for their vacations!

Finland has become a rest haven, a shopper's paradise, and a recreational retreat for thousands of visitors every year. Even the Soviets make pilgrimages to the country, which was once a grand duchy of Imperial Russia. They especially like to visit Turku, where Lenin, one of the fathers of the Communist revolution in Russia, hid out after one of his early failures. The flow of German marks, Soviet rubles, Swedish kronor, and other European currency gives Finland a strong financial base in the world's leisure market.

North American tourists are just as welcome. The Finns are always glad to see visitors from the United States and Canada. It seems as if almost everyone has a relative on the west side of the Atlantic Ocean. The migrating Finns of years past were looking for homesteads much like those they left behind. Finns searched for and found homes in Michigan (where they founded Suomi College), Wisconsin, Minnesota, and Ontario, where the woods and water reminded them of the Old Country. John Morton, of Finnish descent, cast the deciding vote that gave the United States its Declaration of Independence.

Finland is 70 percent forest covered, with more than sixty thousand major lakes. It is an outdoors country, with a people who love the freshness of new things.

Surprising and wonderful new things happen during the day's slow beginnings in the center of Helsinki, Finland's capital city. The dawn seems to take ages to grow into morning during the slow Helsinki summer. A faint pinkness appears in the sky about 2:00 A.M., streaking the horizon over the bay and bouncing beams from the cathedral domes. It hangs on with its half-light for several more hours, disturbing the mind's time clock, which says it should not be so bright so early.

Russian vacationers in Finland enjoy visiting Turku, on the banks of the Aura River.

*The waters of the Töölönlahti Lagoon are glass smooth
in the misty half-light of Helsinki's long summer dawn.*

The water of the Töölönlahti Lagoon at this hour lies glass
smooth. With the shoreline barely wave-washed, a duck family
putt-putts out from its hiding place in search of breakfast.

In the harbor, a wisp of mist floats around the moorings. It
tickles the edges of the giant ferryboats that can crunch through
winter's massive ice jams. But in summer, those greeting the
morning don't think about snow.

There's unexpected pleasure as well in the Turku museum
dedicated to Jean Sibelius, one of Finland's greatest composers. A
visitor can sit in a chair at the little concert hall there, feeling the
sunlight stream in through skylight and windows while listening
to one of the composer's soaring melodies.

There's room for 36,000 islands on Lake Saimaa, in southeast
Finland. The graceful white cruise ship *Kristina Brahe* cuts through
the tan-colored water on its way northward to Savonlinna. The
lake is larger than the combined areas of The Netherlands
(Holland) and Belgium, with a shoreline that could encircle the
equator one and a half times. Rays from the midday sun bounce
from the ship's foaming wake in an explosion of diamonds.

The cruise ship Kristina Brahe cuts through the waters of Lake Saimaa on its way to Savonlinna.

Enormous log rafts float past on their way to mills at the south end of the lake. Occasionally a small motorboat moves out from a cottage pier on one of the islands. Those on board cheer and wave at the tourists, who shout back their hellos.

In the northern third of the nation, a district known as Lapland, winter roars in hard and cold. For those unused to such weather, it can be unexpected indeed. The darkness lasts for almost two months, with only a washed-out moon to light the frozen tundra. However, the aurora borealis (northern lights), a spectacular display of electrical colors in the sky, often sparkles across the dim landscape.

The Lapps—who prefer to be called Samis—are a migratory people. Most of them herd reindeer in Lapland, swallowed by its vast open space. But then, out of the darkness, springs the modern city of Rovaniemi, the district capital—yet another Finnish surprise. It is a brand-new town, with wide streets and solid buildings.

Finland's many contrasts are delightful, refreshing, and exciting. They certainly make the country a land of unexpected enchantment.

Lapland in the autumn

Chapter 2

THE RUGGED LAND

Finland is one of the most northern countries in the world. Long and narrow, it stretches to within 1,370 miles (2,204 kilometers) of the North Pole. About one third of Finland lies north of the Arctic Circle. A straight line drawn from the top to the bottom of the country would be 720 miles (1,159 kilometers) long. From its eastern border with the Soviet Union to the western border at the Gulf of Bothnia, it is 335 miles (539 kilometers) wide at its widest part.

Finland is one of the larger countries in Europe — in area, if not in population. Only France, Sweden, the Soviet Union, and Spain are bigger. Finland encompasses about 130,094 square miles (336,943 square kilometers), which makes it larger than the British Isles. As an independent nation, Finland is very young. But geologists say that Finland's geographic backbone is ancient. Its oldest rocks are more than 29 million years old, and the youngest are at least 18 million years old.

Finland used to be very mountainous. Yet the passage of time has worn down those old hills, which are called *fells*. Erosion from wind and rain and passing glaciers have given Finland a gently rolling landscape. This occurred even before the last ice age, twelve thousand years ago, which spread a frosty blanket over the entire landscape.

LAKES, TREES, AND ROCKS

As the weight and pressure of the melting ice lifted, so did the land. However, in the hollows and valleys of the old forgotten mountains, lakes formed. Offshore, in the Gulf of Finland, the thousands of islands are the remains of some of those ancient peaks. Even today, the land is rising. Scientific studies show that the northern coast rises about 3.25 feet (.99 meters) every century. The southern coast is rising more slowly but just as steadily. Perhaps those ancient mountains are waking up after their long sleep.

The highest point of land in Finland is Mount Haltia on the Norwegian frontier. It is 4,357 feet (1,328 meters) above sea level. However, the land averages barely 550 feet (168 meters) above sea level. But that does not mean Finland is flat. There are enough boulders and rocks piled up to delight a giant. The surface of the landscape has been knocked around by nature for so long that it appears to be bleak and forlorn. The many trees soften that rough texture, covering everything with a rich green fur.

Finns say that their country without trees would be like a bear without its skin. The green forests flow over the ground like a tide. Oak, willow, maple, and alder can be found, mostly in southern and central Finland. Pine, spruce, and birch stretch northward past the Arctic Circle. Without the protection of its "green fur," Finland's soil would long ago have blown away. The forestry industry is the mainstay of the country's economy.

The forests of Finland have been cleared in many places so that the fertile soil can be used for growing crops.

The thousands of Finnish lakes are dotted with tree-covered islands.

The coastal plain, stretching inland from the gulfs of Finland and Bothnia, has been cleared of many trees. Its fertile soil is now being used for growing crops.

The more than sixty thousand lakes in Finland are not set in neat circles across the face of the country. They are ragged and jagged, connected to each other by open waterways. From the deck of a boat, it's often hard to tell how large each lake is. Only from an airplane can one get a good view of the Finnish lakes. Water is everywhere, dotted with tree-covered islands. There aren't as many lakes in Lapland, but there are more swamps.

This pretty pattern of lakes, trees, and rocks is repeated all along the Finnish coast. Thousands of islands in the southwest form what is called an archipelago, lying like stepping-stones across the Baltic Sea. The sea sneaks up on the land in many inlets and bays. It's impossible to tell exactly the length of the Finnish coastline because of the endless indentations made by the water. Mapmakers take the easy way out. They say that the coast is "between 700 and 3,000 miles" (1,126 and 4,827 kilometers) long, speaking generally about the stretch from the southeast around to the northwest. Nobody can be sure—because if every little cut in the land and every bit of beach around each of the 32,000 offshore islands were added up, there would probably be more than 20,000 miles (32,180 kilometers) of coastline!

A SURPRISING CLIMATE

It is not as cold in Finland as its geography might indicate. Warm air currents blow across the country from the coast of Norway, where the North Atlantic Current surges. The Baltic Sea to the south also tends to promote milder temperatures.

Snow blankets the landscape during Finland's long winters.

February is the coldest month of the year. The Finns call February the "pearl month" because of the frosty whiteness all around. During the winter, the temperatures often fall below zero. Low temperatures are usually accompanied by blue skies and sunshine bright enough to dazzle the eyes. The days are very short. The sun comes up about 9:30 A.M. and sets just after 3:00 P.M. Days get shorter the farther north you go. During the summer, the reverse is true. More than seventy-three days of continuous daylight can be observed in the far north. People put black shades on their windows so they can get to sleep during the "sunny" summer nights.

During the autumn, rain and snow make life miserable. The snow and sleet usually become slushy, and children catch colds

In the spring, wild flowers seem to blossom overnight and Arctic cloudberries spring up everywhere.

very easily during these messy days. October is unhappily called the "mud month." So everyone is excited when winter finally comes with its frigid air and fresh snow.

Spring bursts across the country in a blast of colors. It seems as if all the buds begin to blossom overnight. Finns love flowers, and many houses have flower boxes on windowsills or rainbow-hued gardens nearby. In spring, the air is heavy with the scent of blooms. Wild strawberries and blueberries, Arctic bramble and cloudberries spring up everywhere.

July is called "hay month" because it is harvest time. Finland's people love heading for the country during the lazy days of summer. Vacation cottages on islands or deep in the forests make it easy for city folk to forget the bustle of downtown life.

STRONG, SILENT TYPES

The Finnish landscape has shaped the Finns as well. It has been said that the change from the harsh white cold of winter to the gold and green of summer is like the personality of the Finns. They are very reflective people. Their moods swing widely from happiness to sadness. But once you become a friend, they are very generous. There are many stories about the Finnish personality, especially tales about how quiet Finns are.

One legend tells of a farmer who was certain that his son had been born deaf and unable to speak. For twenty years, the son didn't say a thing. Then, while the two were working in a field, they broke their plow against a rock. "Darn it!" said the son. The father was amazed that he had finally spoken. "Why didn't you talk before?" he asked. The younger man replied, "I just didn't have anything to say until now."

The Finnish people aren't really quite as silent as that story might make you believe. But they often would rather observe what is going on in the world than comment on it. They are a very brave people, with a national trait that is called *sisu*. You could say that *sisu* means "backbone," or the refusal to give up when things get tough. Finns have shown this trait over the many years they have had to fight for their country and their ideals.

The Finns love the world of nature. Until recently, the forests supplied almost everything for their lives, from wood for homes, furniture, boats, and wagons to the wild animals that still roam there. In the early days, the Finns traded skins for food.

Even today, that outdoor influence is still evident. The word for money, *raha*, comes from the Finnish term for animal fur. Remember that moose—or was it an elk?—that ran in front of the

A trail in a Finnish forest

cars? Those large animals can be seen even close to the big cities. Lynx and bear often are observed in the back country. Wolves sometimes have been reported in the far northern regions of Finland. And everywhere are the trees.

Of course, as is true of many countries, the cities in Finland are expanding. Industry is growing, as is the fear of pollution. Yet you don't have to go far from the cities before the expanse of forest closes in again. Since most of the people live in the southwestern part of the country, fewer and fewer people can be found as you go northward.

The Finns are calmed and refreshed by the country they love so much. It stretches their imaginations and gives them space to think. They don't have a lot of ancient buildings or a fat national history book on which to dwell. They prefer their natural ties to the land and what it offers them.

Chapter 3

HISTORY'S
CAT-AND-MOUSE GAME

People have been living in Finland since the melting of the last great ice shelf that covered the country. That was at least twelve thousand years ago. It is believed that the ancestors of today's Finns arrived on the shores of the Gulf of Finland from the Volga River area of Russia. These people were mostly hunters, trappers, and fishermen who stayed along the coast. The interior of the country was already occupied by the ancestors of the Sami, the nomadic Lapps of Finland who still retain many of their ancient traditions.

Some of the people who migrated to Finland had split off thousands of years earlier and moved farther south to the warmer lands of what is now Hungary. They eventually became known as Magyars, or Hungarians. Others remained in Estonia, on the southeastern end of the Baltic Sea. Finnish, Estonian, and Hungarian belong to the same Finno-Ugric (Uralic and Altaic) family of languages. But, despite their common origin, it is still hard for the nationalities to understand each other's languages.

When the ancestors of today's Finns arrived on the shores of the Gulf of Finland, the interior of the country (opposite) was already occupied by ancestors of the Sami, the nomadic Lapps of Finland.

Even in the time of Roman historian Tacitus, the Lapps were reindeer herders.

Archaeologists have found ceramic pieces from broken eating dishes dating from 4000 B.C. in many places along the shores of the Gulf of Finland. About 2000 B.C., traders came into contact with the people who lived there. They used flint for arrowheads and amber for jewelry. Other immigrants arrived, bringing with them experience in farming and raising cattle.

Almost two thousand years ago, the Roman historian Tacitus described a wild tribe he called the "Fenni," who supposedly moved from place to place throughout the north. They ate only grass, he said. He might have been describing the Lapps, rather than the more settled tribes along the coast. However, most likely he was simply repeating tall tales told by other travelers. The Lapps were actually reindeer herders even then and had an advanced culture for their time.

At the beginning of the Christian era, more people moved into

Finland from Estonia. They brought with them the use of iron. Farming and cultural contacts expanded in this time as well. This melding of the old tribes with the new arrivals became the ethnic basis for today's modern Finn. At the same time, people moved to the west coast and southwestern Finland from west of the Gulf of Bothnia. These people spoke Swedish. Thus, the two official national languages of present Finland—Finnish and Swedish—both were introduced over a thousand years ago.

Yet the Finns were separated from the rest of Europe. Their language, customs, and culture set them apart. Two other details would plague the Finns for their entire history. They lived in a small, but strategically located, country. It was also very rich in natural resources. For those reasons, Finland was often invaded. It was almost as if Finland were a mouse being chased by all the big cats of Europe—most of all, by Russia and Sweden. But the tough nature of the Finns helped them survive as a people through all those bloody generations.

SWEDISH RULE

Missionaries brought the Finnish tribes into closer contact with the rest of Europe. The churchmen arrived in the middle of the eleventh century, basing their activities in the Åland Islands. In the twelfth century, Swedish King Erik IX had his eye on expanding his territory. He believed that Finland would make a good province. King Erik disguised his intentions by calling his invasion a crusade to convert pagans. Erik sent in English-born Bishop Henry of Uppsala to pave the way. But this energetic fellow didn't receive a friendly welcome. According to one story, a Finnish farmer used his axe to hack Henry to death when they

The Swedes built Turku castle in the Middle Ages. It is one of the two surviving medieval buildings in what was then the capital city.

were walking across a frozen lake. It took quite a while before other missionaries cared to go to Finland. But eventually they came in greater numbers—with soldiers for protection. So Sweden gained a province, and most of the Finns were Christianized.

Good Henry was made the patron saint of Finland, which gave the Finnish church a heavenly protector. What happened to King Erik? He was made patron saint of Sweden!

Thus Finland was ushered into a long period of Swedish rule. It took the Swedes several generations, though, to move inland from the western coasts. Finland was officially named a Swedish province in 1362, with the right to participate in Swedish royal elections. The Finns also had to pay taxes, but they were permitted to sit in on meetings of the Swedish *riksdag* (parliament).

The Swedes built many castles and strongholds around the country as they extended their rule. The areas around the forts were called "castle country," or *linnanlanni*. The most important of these was Turku on the southwest coast. Visitors can still see the old fort, which has been the setting for numerous movies in recent years.

Another important town was Viipuri, which had trade links with the Hanseatic League cities of northern Europe. These were free towns with large merchant and banking populations. They controlled much of the economy during the Middle Ages. Most Finns still lived in small villages, however, well away from the larger coastal cities.

The relationship between the Swedish and Finnish churches was a major unifying tie between the two countries. The bishop of Turku was a very powerful figure in those days. He perhaps had even more control over the Finns than did the local aristocracy.

Many of the resident dukes and princes were foreigners, and the natives didn't care much for them.

This Swedish-Finnish relationship lasted more than six hundred years. It was not always good for Finland. The country became a buffer for Sweden, which wanted to protect itself from attack from the east. Finland, therefore, often found itself fighting wars that were not its own. In 1495, for instance, Sweden wanted to break away from a union with Denmark and Norway. Denmark objected and asked its ally, Russia, to attack Finland, because Finland was a province of Sweden. That was only one of at least forty times that Finland has found itself at war with Russia.

HARD TIMES

In the Thirty Years War (1618-1648), Finland fought with Sweden against Russia. The war was a great burden for Finland. More than eighteen thousand Finnish soldiers had to join the army each year; they were respected and feared fighters. The Finnish cavalry was known as the *hackapelites*. The name came from their battle cry, *Hakkaa päälle!* which meant "Get to 'em!"

Finland was hit even harder during the Great Northern War, which dragged on from 1700 to 1721. The Finns had a harsher term for it, calling the conflict the "Great Wrath." Peter the Great was ruling Russia then. He sent his mounted cossacks, who were fierce warriors, all across Finland. More than 100,000 Finns were killed in the resulting battles, which were followed by famine and disease. Almost one fourth of the entire Finnish population died. Despite the carnage, Russia was able to capture only a small slice of Finnish territory in the southeast. Sweden still ruled the rest of the country.

This constant threat from Russia frightened some Finns. Their military men, especially, knew they had little chance against the greater power of their eastern neighbor. In 1788, a group of officers proposed that Finland secede from Sweden and become an independent country under the protection of Russia. The revolt was quickly put down.

Yet by the mid-eighteenth century, much of the warfare had died down, resulting in an economic and population boom for Finland. There was a period in which culture and trade expanded and more contact was made with the rest of Europe.

THE QUEST FOR FREEDOM

During these bloody years, native Finns and even Swedish-Finns resented the interference of other countries in their affairs. They began to work for independence. The quest for freedom extended over many years and involved many famous Finns.

Henrik Gabriel Porthan, a university professor, wrote a Finnish-language grammar book. In it he argued that Finland was a separate nation. Great patriotic poems flowed from the pen of Johan Ludvig Runeberg. Philosopher Johan Wilhelm Snellman argued for a free Finland. "We are not Swedes, we don't want to be Russians, so let's be Finns," insisted Adolf Ivar Arwidsson.

But Finland remained firmly in the Swedish camp. In 1556, Finland was made a grand duchy of Sweden by Gustavus Vasa, who installed his son John as grand duke. Finland, like the rest of Europe, was swept up in the religious wars of the time. The Protestant Reformation had begun, and Catholic princes fought non-Catholic princes all over Europe. Sweden fought against countries that remained with the Catholic church, which again meant that Finnish soldiers were drafted to fight in wars they didn't have any personal benefit from.

But with the church split, Finland acquired a national language; the Bible was translated into the local speech and was widely distributed. Hymnals and other religious writings also were printed. Yet a knowledge of Swedish was important for anyone wishing to enter government service or to become a merchant.

RUSSIAN RULE

By this time, the Swedish empire was declining at the edges. The country was not strong enough to control its once-expansive territories. In 1807, Russia's Tsar Alexander I and France's Napoleon I signed a secret agreement that gave Russia the "right" to annex Finland. Of course, no one asked the Finns how they felt about this. The Swedes didn't like it either. The result was — inevitably — another war.

Alexander found an excuse to invade Finland. The resulting war lasted a year and a half, ending in September, 1809. The Swedish army was chased into the northern forests, where many soldiers died. Out of desperation, the Swedes signed a peace treaty that gave up all rights to Finland and the Åland Islands. Finland thus became a grand duchy of Russia.

At least, the Finns thought, this was better than being attacked by the Russians almost every other year. Since they didn't like being the revolving door for other countries' armies, they were happy to have peace. Tsar Alexander tried hard to make the Finns feel comfortable. He gave them almost as many rights and privileges as they had had under Swedish rule. He even let them keep their Lutheran church and the Swedish-based legal system.

This statue of poet Johan Ludvig Runeberg has an honored place on the Esplanade in a lovely Helsinki park.

Although the tsar called himself the Grand Duke of Finland, he let the Finns administer their own affairs—a generous attitude for that time. Yet even these favors weren't enough. Many Finns still wanted to be independent. The publication in 1835 of the Finnish national folk epic, the *Kalevala,* made the people conscious of their heritage. It inspired them to work harder for independence.

Poet Johan Ludvig Runeberg and novelist Zacharias Topelius also favored freedom for Finland. They both wrote in Swedish. In 1846, Runeberg wrote the poem "Our Land," which became the Finnish national anthem. Swedish remained the official language of Finland, even under Russian rule. Yet, in 1863, through the efforts of many patriots, the Finnish language finally was granted equal status in the courts and in the legal system.

The university in Turku, later moved to Helsinki, became very important, turning out hundreds of scholars, administrators, businessmen, and clergymen. Most of the leaders in Finland's

Tsar Nicholas II of Russia took power in 1894 and became a much stricter administrator of Finland than previous tsars had been.

fight for freedom were graduated from Turku and went on to achieve many great things for their country.

Many Finns also went into the imperial Russian army. The Russians even gave the Finns their own cadet school. Hundreds reached the ranks of general and admiral. When they retired or returned to civilian life, they brought their expertise in governmental affairs with them.

The Russians improved the industrial base of Finland and built waterways and railroads. Finnish forests became important to the nation's economy. Wood was used to build ships, homes, and factories. The Russians let the Finns have their own system of currency, which in turn resulted in a great deal of economic freedom.

However, toward the end of the nineteenth century, the Russians had a change of heart. They became afraid of the growing independence of the Finns. Russian was declared the official language in some branches of government service, and Russian-born civil servants were put in charge of important duties in Finland. A new tsar, Nicholas II, assigned a gruff, tough governor-general to oversee the Finns. Nikolai Ivanovich Bobrikov didn't care what the Finns thought of him and stripped a lot of power from the Finnish parliament. Freedom of speech, assembly, and the press were cut back.

*While Governor-General Nikolai Ivanovich Bobrikov looks on
(far right), Tsar Nicholas II (leaning on table) signs away most of
Finland's liberties.*

Though the Finns hated Bobrikov, they did not protest; they
simply did not comply. But one day in 1904, a Finnish civil
servant named Eugen Schauman shot and killed the governor. The
Russians then tried to crack down even harder, but they were
shaken at home by the peasants' revolution of 1905. They also
were involved in a war with Japan. Eventually, the tsar had to
give back the powers he had taken from the Finnish parliament.
The Finns also were given the right to vote for their
representatives, making theirs the most democratic legislature in
Europe at the time.

Unfortunately, this relief didn't last long. World War I broke
out in August, 1914. The Russians, afraid of what the Finns might
do, kept a tight rein on the Finnish parliament. Thousands of
young Finns fled to Germany and fought for that country,
believing that if Germany defeated Russia, Finland would be free.
Others conspired against Russia by assisting leftists such as the
Communists, who were seeking to overthrow the tsar.

When Tsar Nicholas was deposed in 1917, the Finns rejoiced.
They declared their independence on December 6 of that same
year. But still Finland was not quite totally free of problems.

The General Carl Gustav Mannerheim statue in Helsinki

Chapter 4

FROM CIVIL WAR
TO MODERN STATE

The new rulers of Russia were Communists called Bolsheviks. They recognized the independent nation of Finland. But before a government could be established, Finland had to endure a short, but fierce, civil war. The Finnish "Reds" attempted to set up a socialist government similar to that which had taken over in Russia. The Finnish "Whites" felt that under socialism Finland would still be controlled by their larger neighbor.

The Reds were aided by Russian troops, while the Whites were helped by Germans and Finns who had been trained in Germany. The White commander, General Carl Gustav Mannerheim, a former general in the tsar's army, didn't appreciate the German assistance. He felt that outside powers had no business in Finnish affairs. But he really had no choice. The Communist government in Russia was pouring more soldiers into the Red camp. The other White commanders felt they needed all the assistance they could get, regardless of the source.

The Reds captured Helsinki, Finland's capital, in January, 1918, causing the parliament to flee. In April, Mannerheim won a decisive battle over the Reds and with the help of the Germans retook Helsinki. By May, the war was over. The Whites had won. The superior training of their officers and troops had made the big difference. Thousands had died on both sides, causing bitter feelings that still remain today.

A NEW CONSTITUTION

When the war ended, Germany wanted Finland to remain under its influence. Germany supported right-wing politicians, who took over the Finnish parliament. They sought to keep Finland a monarchy. Kaiser Wilhelm II of Germany suggested that his son-in-law would make a fine king. So in October, 1918, the Finnish parliament elected Prince Friedrich Karl of Hesse as Finland's new ruler. However, World War I ended in that November, with the defeat of Germany. Prince Friedrich Karl decided it wouldn't be very wise to be a king after all. Besides, the Finns were having second thoughts. They did not want to trade one foreign ruler for another.

General Mannerheim, who had opposed the whole arrangement with Germany, was asked to oversee the rebuilding of the country. Elections were held, and the majority of Finns voted for a republic. A new constitution was written and Mannerheim signed the document. It established a single-house parliament and a president elected by an electoral college, a group of popularly elected special representatives. The president was to have a six-year term.

When the electoral college voted, they named Kaarlo Juho Ståhlberg as the first president of Finland. He had been a law

Kyösti Kallio was president of Finland from 1937 to 1940.

professor and had written most of the new constitution. In the voting, Mannerheim was defeated, probably because many people with Red ties resented him for his military actions during the civil war. Mannerheim retired.

In 1920, Finland signed a treaty with Russia. However, the majority of Finns still feared the Bolsheviks.

In 1930, the right-wing Lapua Movement succeeded in having the Communist party banned in Finland. After this success, they tried to take over the government, but failed. There were many street fights; meetings on both sides were broken up by armed mobs. The friction brought back memories of the civil war. It was not until the late 1930s that the Finns put their internal disputes aside—in the face of an even greater threat.

In 1938, Russia, now being called the Soviet Union, asked permission to build a military base on Finnish territory. It claimed the base was needed for protection against the rising power of Nazi Germany. The Finns refused to bargain, especially when their neighbor suggested that some of their common borders be shifted around. But Finland's future was sealed when the Germans and the Soviets pretended to be friends and signed a treaty in 1939. The pact all but gave Finland to the Soviet Union.

THE WINTER WAR

The Finns wouldn't give up any of their land. So the Soviet Union invaded Finland on November 30, 1939. They didn't even declare war, expecting to smash the little country right away. They also thought those who remembered the terrors of the civil war would be willing to fight for the Reds again. But they hadn't counted on *sisu,* the courage of the Finns.

The country united to fight off the attack. Instead of sweeping through the country as planned, the Soviets made no headway against the stubborn Finns. But it was an unequal struggle in terms of equipment and manpower. The Finns had only forty tanks; the Soviets had two thousand. The Finns had no air force; the Soviets controlled the skies. The Finns had to use captured weapons; the Soviets had unlimited weapons and ammunition.

But the Finns were fighting for their own country. They were led by Mannerheim, who had come out of retirement. They also were helped by one of the worst winters in Finnish history, which bogged down the Soviet attack. Temperatures plunged to minus 40 degrees Fahrenheit (minus 40 degrees Celsius) and deep snow covered the countryside. Finnish soldiers, disguised in white uniforms, skied at will around the battlefields. The Soviet troops (who wore dark uniforms) couldn't even see them.

The rest of the world admired the courage of the Finns, but no nation sent any help. So the Finns hung on for more than three months before being slowly battered to their knees. The Soviets were just as happy to call it quits when the Finns finally agreed to talk.

Neither side won and neither lost. It was a stalemate, but one that favored the larger Soviet Union. That country was able to demand huge chunks of Finnish territory in exchange for ending the conflict. The Finns had to swallow their pride, giving up about a tenth of their land, which included Viipuri, the country's second-largest city.

THE CONTINUATION WAR

Barely more than a year later, the Finns found themselves drawn into yet another conflict. They were swept up into the horrors of World War II, which they called "The Continuation War." With the German conquest of Denmark and Norway, Finland felt isolated against the threats of the Soviet Union. Nazi Germany seemed to be the only power strong enough to keep the Soviets away. The Finns therefore agreed to let German troops cross their country to reach northern Norway.

Finland wanted to remain neutral. But though they hated the Nazis, the Finns felt they couldn't afford to refuse the German demands. Adolf Hitler, the leader of the Nazis, took advantage of the pact with Finland to plan an attack on the Soviet Union. Soon thousands of German troops were in Finland. The Finns, however, refused to do much fighting when Germany attacked the Soviet Union in 1941. When the Finns did fight the Soviets, they felt it was merely a continuation of their Winter War.

By the summer of 1944, it was obvious that the Germans were going to lose. The Soviets had moved farther and farther into Finland. In order to head off a total Soviet takeover of their country, Finland agreed to an armistice.

Under the terms of the agreement, the Finns promised to drive out the Nazi troops still on their soil. It took months to do that, and the retreating Germans destroyed everything in sight. The Soviets also took control of more large chunks of Finnish territory, including some of the richest mineral deposits and best ports.

This time, the Finns had indeed lost. But again, their *sisu* held firm. Despite Soviet demands for heavy reparations, the country was able to rebuild itself and pay back its war debts. Mannerheim, who had been elected president of Finland in 1944, resigned in 1946 because of ill health. He was succeeded by Dr. Juho K. Paasikivi. Under Paasikivi's direction, Finland was neutral and did not take sides in the conflict between the Western nations and those of the East under Soviet control.

A NEUTRAL COUNTRY

After World War II, the Finns adopted a policy of neutrality. They agree that it's wise to follow a governmental policy that is in the best interest of Finland. The main objective of their neutrality is that Finland remain an independent republic and maintain friendly relations with her neighbors, particularly the Soviet Union and the other Scandinavian countries. The Finns feel that by doing so they can best serve the citizens of Finland and work for world peace.

Finland takes an active part in world politics by taking peace initiatives. The Finns, for example, originally proposed the

Finlandia Hall, Helsinki's conference center, has been the site of many meetings between democratic and communist countries.

European Security Conference. In honor of that fact, the final session and the signing of the Helsinki Accords of 1975 were held in the Finnish capital. The Finns often have offered their cities as sites for meetings between countries with different political systems. The nation also has hosted tne Soviet-American Strategic Arms Limitation Talks (SALT) — discussions about reducing the number of weapons on both sides. Finland's neutrality thus makes it possible for the Finns to help in the efforts for world peace. The Finns are also members of the United Nations and proudly and bravely speak up when they see the need.

Some outsiders might not agree with what the Finns call

Dr. Urho Kekkonen served as president of Finland from 1956 until his retirement in 1981.

neutrality. They think the Soviet Union still plays too strong a role in Finnish politics. Finland is the only Western democratic neighbor that shares a long border with the Soviet Union. The Soviets are, however, content to let the Finns alone. It is important to them that Finland is neutral, because that helps ensure that Sweden also will remain neutral. Thus, that part of the world will stay relatively quiet and stable.

Deftly overseeing all this juggling was the then-president of Finland, Dr. Urho Kekkonen. He was first elected in 1956 and reelected in 1968, 1974, and 1978. Kekkonen resigned because of ill health and advanced age after serving for twenty-five years as head of his country. Despite his continuing leadership, the Finns agree that it often has been difficult to get much accomplished in the parliament. In January, 1982, Mauno Koivisto was elected the new president of Finland.

There have been more than twenty governments in Finland since the end of World War I. Some observers have called the Finnish brand of politics "small town stuff"—everybody knows everybody else, and everybody wants to be part of the governing group.

FINLAND'S GOVERNMENT

Let's backtrack a bit for a closer look at the Finnish system of government. Although Finland was part of a monarchy for centuries, it never had its own king. Either the Swedish king or the Russian tsar ruled the land.

In 1906, Finland authorized universal suffrage, which meant that every adult in the country could vote. It thus became the first European country to give women the right to participate in elections. The Finns are very proud of that fact. After World War I, the constitution of the newly independent country declared that Finland was to be a republic, headed by a president.

The president is not supposed to belong to any political party. But the chief executive has far-reaching powers and takes a strong role in international and internal affairs. The president can start legislation and is responsible for approving bills passed by parliament. He also is responsible for appointing the prime minister and the cabinet, as well as bishops and even some university professors.

After the president, the next most important government figure is the prime minister, the *pääministeri,* who is head of the government and chairman of the Council of State, the *valtioneuvosto.* There are usually sixteen or seventeen ministers working with the prime minister, heading various governmental departments. A government "falls" when it has lost the support of parliament. The president must then choose another prime minister.

The parliament, called *Eduskunta,* consists of two hundred representatives (*kansanedustaja*) who are elected by the people for four-year terms. Currently, there are eight political parties

The Council of State Building on Senate Square in Helsinki

represented in the parliament. The major ones are the Social Democrats, the Conservatives, the Center Party (formerly Agrarians), and the Communists.

The parliament has a number of committees that help prepare legislation; for instance, there are the Foreign Affairs Committee, the Bank Committee, and others, including the *suuri valiokunta* (the Grand Committee), which acts as an informal second parliament.

Finland today is divided into twelve provinces, called *lääni*, each headed by a governor appointed by the national president. Each province is run by a board that is not elected but is merely an administrative body. Local government functions are carried out by communes, each with a council elected by the people.

The services provided by communes include paving highways such as this one in Oulu.

There are three different kinds of communes: the rural commune, the market village, and the city. Each provides services for its citizens, from running hospitals to paving roads.

The bigger the commune, the more status it has. Communes can shift officially from one stage to another, in a move based primarily on increase in population. At midnight on December 31, a change of status is officially announced in a commune that has grown in size, for instance, from a market village to the status of a city. There are fireworks, speeches, and parades—even at that late hour.

Many details of the legal system were drawn from Sweden, including a detailed court system of judges and juries. The Supreme Court of Finland is the highest in the land.

The Finns have been able to draw on the best of what they have seen in other countries, shaping and molding governmental forms, laws, and foreign policy to meet their own needs. They've been able to remain relatively independent and strong in the knowledge that Finland has withstood terrible things during its history.

"We're like cats," says one Finn. "We always land on our feet."

Chapter 5

DAUGHTER OF
THE BALTIC

The waters of the Töölönlahti Lagoon are quiet in the Helsinki dawn. The end of the half-night that marks a Finnish summer has crept over the city. The sun dropped behind the horizon at 11 P.M. and appeared again about 2 A.M., bringing a murky glow that flows over the capital. A loon, whose inner clock isn't jarred by the crazy hours, hoots from somewhere on the north bank of this lake in the city's center. Another bird answers from its perch along the commuter railroad line on the opposite shore.

Nobody seems to be awake yet. Everything is quiet, until an early taxi swooshes past, its tires whispering across the wet pavement. But the stillness doesn't last long. The first vegetable vendors are already setting up their stalls in the marketplace. More farmers are arriving at the wide square along the waterfront where they will sell their beets, lettuce, onions, and other wares. Flowers explode in bright colors everywhere; breakfast aromas float out of the homes.

Helsinki is finally ready for another day.

*The beginning of a Finnish summer dawn brings
a murky glow to Helsinki's South Harbor.*

Above: A view of Helsinki's South Harbor market, one of the most popular shopping areas in the city. Below: A busy downtown Helsinki street.

Helsinki scenes:
Top: Boats moored
in the harbor.
Above: The South
Harbor flower market.
Left: An aerial view.

The city has been the capital of Finland since 1812, when the Russians took that honor away from Turku, which had been the country's chief city under Swedish rule. Helsinki lies on a hunk of hard rock, jutting out into the cold Baltic Sea. The town is almost surrounded by water. This special relationship with the sea has earned Helsinki the nickname "Daughter of the Baltic." The influence of the water can be felt everywhere, from the damp breeze that sweeps along the wide promenades to the bustling harbor. About 505,000 people live in Helsinki. As is true of many cities, the population growth is mostly in the suburbs.

HELSINKI YESTERDAY

Helsinki was founded in 1550 by a decree of Swedish King Gustavus. He wanted to make a trading center that would take business away from other cities in the Baltic area. Not many people wanted to live on the rocky, windswept peninsula he chose as the site of the town. But Gustavus was a dictator, and he got what he wanted. He forced people from Rauma, Ulvila, Tammisaari, and Porvoo to move to the new city on the river Vantaa.

At first, Helsinki didn't match the expectations of its founder. The people were angry at being forced to live there, and they all wanted to go back to their original homes. So in 1556, Gustavus allowed the folks from Rauma and Ulvila to return. That left mostly Swedes living in Helsinki. It wasn't until the end of the 1800s that the city had a Finnish majority. Over the subsequent years, the town location was shifted southward to more suitable land.

Yet even the new site wasn't very comfortable. Nor was it the

The eighteenth-century island fortress of Suomenlinna

best time for moving a city to a new neighborhood. There were continual wars, sickness was everywhere, and business people preferred to locate elsewhere. From 1713 to 1721, the place was occupied by Russian soldiers. For some reason, Helsinki had gained a reputation for being a good place to send armies, although it appeared that no civilians really wanted to live there. Numerous battles were fought in the area over the next generation.

It wasn't until the Swedes built the huge island fortress of Suomenlinna in the 1740s that a welcome peace came to Helsinki. Housewives no longer had to worry that their flowerpots would be knocked over by wandering troopers. Best of all, merchants decided after all that the harbor would be a good place to dock their ships. From that time, Helsinki expanded.

The Russians came back in 1808, after defeating the Swedes. Finland became a grand duchy of its eastern neighbor. Much rebuilding was needed in order to make Helsinki the capital. Two architects, Johan Albert Ehrenström and Carl Ludvig Engel, put their heads together to make plans.

The onion-shaped domes of Uspenski Cathedral overlook Helsinki. The ornate altar and many beautiful icons attract a steady stream of visitors.

HELSINKI TODAY

Today's visitor to Helsinki won't see many buildings and homes dating from pre-Russian days. Many fires and battles destroyed those early structures, so Helsinki is actually relatively new. Anybody arriving by ship today is presented with one of the most beautiful views in northern Europe. The solemn, lantern-shaped dome of the Lutheran Cathedral and the onion-shaped roofs of the Orthodox Uspenski Cathedral overlook the town. It is an enchanting mixture of east and west.

The modern Taivallahti Church, carved out of solid rock,
is built of Finnish copper, glass, wood, and granite.

Much modern architecture can be seen in Helsinki. Everyone is very proud of the City Theater and Finlandia Hall, which is the city conference center. The Taivallahti Church (called "The Rock Church") is another interesting sight. It was carved out of solid rock, and takes up almost an entire city block. The 1952 Olympics were held in Helsinki, and many of the sport facilities built then are still used today.

Tapiola, the garden community outside Helsinki, is a model town.

The suburb of Tapiola has been nicknamed the "Garden City of Finland." This was one of the first planned urban communities built after World War II. It has been the model for similar towns around the world. Tapiola was planned and built by Heikki von Hertzen, a lawyer who worried that his fellow Finns would not have enough places to live after the devastation of the war. He said he drew his ideas from Finnish mythology, especially the story of Tapio, the king of the forests, whose home was called Tapiola.

Von Hertzen wanted to preserve the countryside as much as possible, so he would not allow bulldozers to clear the land. Even the trees were chopped down by hand. There are playgrounds, shopping centers, homes, and apartments. Everything in Tapiola is within walking distance of everything else.

The people of Helsinki love their city. However, during the summer, one might think that no one lives there. The residents head to vacation cottages on the archipelago or on the west coast for relaxation.

One of the reasons no one likes to stay away too long, though, is the sports park at Pirkkola, a very busy place year round. It covers more than 120 acres (48.6 hectares), with woods, skiing and hiking trails, a swimming pool, ice rink, and halls for indoor ball games. Helsinki residents don't even have to go far to camp out. There are places to pitch tents on the islands near the city, and two large campgrounds lie within the city limits. Every year they accommodate more than 100,000 overnight guests.

Helsinki is a very international city because of its heritage and its position in the world as a conference host. Young people speak a slang, or pidgin, drawn from Finnish, Swedish, Russian, and English. They can "talk" with visitors from many countries, using only their slang and hand gestures! More than one million people pass through the Helsinki harbor every year. Most are from other countries, in Finland on vacation or business trips.

Another popular spot in the city is the zoo, located on an island called Korkeasaari, just a few minutes by ferryboat from downtown Helsinki.

Politicians don't get much of a break to vacation; they have work to do. The Parliament building is in Helsinki, as is the Council of State Building, which was the residence of the Russian governor-general when Finland was under that country's control. More than 27,500 civil servants and officials congregate in downtown Helsinki every day, mingling with the students from the State University.

Obviously, things get very crowded; Helsinki residents are always complaining about the jammed streets. That's why they appreciate the many parks in town.

TURKU: A TALKATIVE TOWN

Turku is just as exciting as Helsinki. Because of its location at the mouth of the Aura River, which empties into the Gulf of Finland, Turku became a major trading center and was the country's capital under Swedish rule.

Numerous fires in the old days destroyed most of the town buildings, but the city always rebuilt itself and celebrated its 750th birthday in 1979. Its people have a good feeling for the past. There were Iron Age settlements on this spot in western Finland even before anyone thought of founding a city. So Turku is actually much older than its birthday would indicate. Today, about 170,000 people live here.

Many of the residents have Swedish backgrounds. Swedish crusaders marched into town in 1157 and refused to go home. For several hundred years, the city was called by its Swedish name, Åbo, and was the third-largest city in the Swedish empire. It was always politically active, with a large university and a free spirit that encouraged plotters from around the world. For a time, it seemed as if every revolutionary in the world visited Turku for some rest, relaxation, and radicalism.

The subject matter is different now, but Turku's residents still love to talk. They especially enjoy getting together in the coffeehouses along the Östra Strandgatan, a narrow street fronting the Aura River near the Swedish University.

Many Russian tourists enjoy visiting the city that harbored Lenin and other founders of the modern Soviet state who fled from the tsar's police. Western Europeans come for other reasons, most notably for shopping.

Turku's castle, built by the Swedes, is a major tourist attraction.

Lacemaking at the Turku handicrafts museum

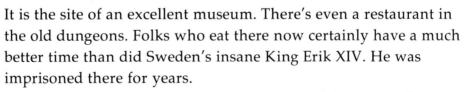

Turku

Helsinki

It is the site of an excellent museum. There's even a restaurant in the old dungeons. Folks who eat there now certainly have a much better time than did Sweden's insane King Erik XIV. He was imprisoned there for years.

The only district that escaped all the fires of the past is the neighborhood called Luostarinmäki (Cloister Hill). It is now a historical site where craft workers ply their trades in the shops. Schoolchildren love to visit the narrow streets and peer into the refurbished homes. A stop at the candy maker's shop is a delicious pause on a class outing.

The modern city of Rovaniemi

LAPLAND: THE FINNISH WILD WEST

Far to the north, away from the soft forests and fields of lower Finland, is Lapland. The tundra stretches from horizon to horizon, and a motorist can drive for hours without seeing another car. Then, suddenly, out of the wilderness pops the modern, totally planned city of Rovaniemi. A former marketplace for Lapp reindeer herders, it was destroyed by the Germans as they retreated from northern Finland during World War II. Architect Alvar Aalto drew up plans for rebuilding the city after the war. It just kept growing after the rubble was cleared away. Rovaniemi now has broad streets, many parks, and new homes. During the winter, most residents ski. In the summer, they fish. There are only a few months in which the owners of small farms can plant and grow their crops. Many farmers have other jobs, usually in the lumber industry.

But the hardy folks who live in Rovaniemi wouldn't want to be anywhere else. It's like the Wild West, or better still, the Wild North of Europe.

The city of Lappeenranta

FINLAND'S PLAYGROUND

Exotic eastern Finland, in the district of Karelia, is very different from the far north. It has more trees, a more diversified economy, and is the playground for the urban dwellers who flock here in the summer. In addition, it borders the Soviet Union. The influence of Russian culture is also very evident in the style of architecture, the language, and the life-style of the people.

Four cities in Karelia give a varied picture of life there. They include Lappeenranta, Imatra, Savonlinna, and Kuopio, each with a different personality. Lappeenranta, about thirteen miles northeast of Helsinki, is on the edge of the most extensive network of lakes in Europe. All the youngsters in town know exactly where the best fishing spots are—they visit them all the time. And why not? Water is everywhere. The city is the commercial center of Karelia and is the terminal point for the Saimaa Canal. The canal links Helsinki with Leningrad, in Russia.

61

Olavinlinna Castle, an island fortress built in the fifteenth century, is the site of the Savonlinna Opera Festival.

Imatra is smaller. But it has the largest timber operation in Europe. Sawmills are going night and day. A *koski,* or waterfall, splashes near the center of town. The Russians used to love Imatra because of the beautiful scenery. They built a spa for the gentry, who enjoyed soaking in what they considered healthful waters.

One of the prettiest drives in Finland is from Imatra to Savonlinna. The road climbs over the Punkaharju Ridge, a narrow neck of rock between two huge lakes. However, many people prefer taking cruise ships across Lake Saimaa.

Savonlinna appears out of the forests like an oasis. It is an old town with winding streets that always seem to end at Lake Saimaa. In fact, Savonlinna is called the "Pearl of the Saimaa." It is a lively harbor town and eastern Finland's biggest spa. But the town's greatest claim to fame is the summer opera festival held in the courtyard of Olavinlinna Castle. This fortress was built in 1475, but its use is much more peaceful now. Long rows of hard green benches fill the area where troops once assembled.

The ornate cupola of Rauhanlinna, the "Castle of Peace"

It is quite a sight to see the opera singers in such major productions as *Boris Godunov*. The colorfully costumed performers fit in very well with the surroundings. But the benches do become uncomfortable during a long program. People who have been there before are wise enough to bring a seat cushion or two! Local people of all ages work on the festival, from setting up the stage to performing on it. Major stars from all over the world are eager to come to Savonlinna because it is such an exciting place in which to perform.

Just outside Savonlinna is the former home of Nils Agaton Weckman, who served in the Russian imperial army. Hundreds of Finnish and Russian workers built this elaborate house in 1896. It is called the "Castle of Peace," or Rauhanlinna, and cost more than

Everywhere in Finland are tiny hotels and guest cottages for vacationers.

200,000 pieces of gold to construct. Now it is a museum, open for tours. If a visitor is very quiet, it's almost possible to hear ghostly waltzes in the grand ballroom.

Not too far from Savonlinna is Kuopio, another major town on the Saimaa Canal. Visitors can climb to the top of the 250-foot-tall Puijo Observation Tower and look over miles of Finnish countryside. It's fun to eat in the restaurant at the top of the tower and watch the birds. The restaurant, reached by an elevator, slowly revolves completely once an hour.

Kuopio is a soccer-crazy town in the spring and fall. It is the site for such international winter sporting events as the Puijo skiing competition each March.

Of course, there are many other towns and villages in Finland, each with its own way of doings things and with its own outlook on life. Everywhere are tiny hotels and guest houses. The Finns enjoy their vacations and jealously guard their time away from

Haikko Manor, once home of poet Johan Ludvig Runeberg, has been converted to a conference center, hotel, and gourmet restaurant.

the job. In addition to Rauhanlinna, other country homes built during the era of the tsars are scattered about the countryside. Many have been turned into holiday hideaways.

Closer to Helsinki is Haikko Manor, once the home of the poet Runeberg, who wrote the words of the Finnish national anthem. It is now a well-known hotel and one of the larger conference centers in the country. The old stables at the manor have been converted to a restaurant that specializes in gourmet fare, such as reindeer meat prepared in several different ways. Haikko Manor is full of antiques, but a modern health spa has been added to help guests unwind after lengthy talks about weighty subjects.

Finland carefully blends the natural, forested world into its urban landscape. The people have a definite love for the land, for the old ways, and for the need to have them come together beautifully. That's just one more reason why the Finns are so proud of their nation.

This birch forest is a sample of Finland's "green gold."

Chapter 6

LAND OF THE

GREEN GOLD

Finland is one of the northernmost countries in the world. It is also one of the largest countries in Europe, at least in landmass. The Finns make up only a fraction of the world's population, but it's been said that 40 percent of all people living north of the Arctic Circle are Finns. Norway and Sweden are mountainous. Finland is flat and marshy—lakes take up 10 percent of its land.

What else is there about Finland that makes it different from other countries? That's easy. Aside from all those lakes, the rest of Finland appears to be nothing but a waving carpet of trees, a living ocean of branches. The forests are the "green gold" of Finland. Those millions and millions of trees—so many that even a magical giant couldn't count them—are the country's most appreciated resource. Some nations have oil fields, others have diamond mines. Trees are Finland's gift from nature. The country has a lumber industry that accounts for almost three quarters of its exports. Finnish wood is used for everything from toothpicks to chairs, buildings to toys. And that means BIG business.

Finnish lumberjacks know that their wood will be made into more products than simply planks. Finnish industries use wood in a variety of ways. The production of wood paneling is very important. The demand for pulp is very high. Another major business makes newsprint, printing and writing papers, and other paper products. Many businesses—from shipping to cabinetmaking—are spin-offs from lumber production.

The forest has been friendly to the Finns since the first tribes made their way into the country. They had to chop down thickets to clear land for their fields. They hid in the woods when enemies threatened. So the Finns loved their forests; they scribbled poems about the forests, they wrote songs and symphonies about the forests. These were the homes of the ancient Finnish gods. The Finn cannot be separated from that green landscape. The spruce, pine, and birch are part of the Finnish soul—and mean more than just sticks to chop down and sell.

Wood in many forms has contributed to the development of Finland. Supposedly, the first Finnish exports in the Middle Ages were bows made from yew trees. Exports of wood tar from the seventeenth to the nineteenth centuries brought needed goods to Finland in exchange. Masts and spars for ships were produced generations ago, as were wooden dishes. The sawmill industry began to grow in the 1870s, the paper industry in the 1880s, and the pulp industry in the 1890s. Most of the products in those days were sold to Russia. Today, the world is Finland's market.

PROTECTING THE FORESTS

The Finns realize that they must take care of their forests. They are very concerned about the environment and know the value of

Finland's forests are the country's most important natural resource.

renewing this precious resource. As early as the seventeenth century, the Finns recognized that if they weren't careful, they might destroy the very product that made their country so special. Then along came the Industrial Revolution; factories sprang up everywhere. There was an explosive demand for wood. A special government bureau was set up in 1859 to guard against too much cutting in Finland's forests.

The Central Forestry Board was founded in 1907 to make sure all timber companies coordinated the harvesting and marketing of wood. Today, most of the forest land is still owned by individuals—some 300,000 landowners. (The National Board of Forests owns only about 25 percent of the forest land; cities and religious congregations own 4 percent; and forest-industry companies own 7 percent.) The average size of the holdings is about 86 acres (34.8 hectares). So you can see that forestry in Finland is mostly private and small-scale.

The Finns have a very strong program of replanting trees to replace those that have been cut down. Without that plan, in just a few years Finland would probably look as if it had been plucked bald.

In addition to reforestation, as the replanting is called, scientists are always looking for other ways to use wood; even sawdust and scrap can be utilized in various ways. Now, many of the loggers simply abandon the branches, stumps, and crowns of the trees they cut. So the forest industry is attempting to figure out what to do with all the leftovers.

There is probably about 25 percent more available wood left behind after the tree harvesting. The government is looking for an economical method of getting all that leftover wood out of the forest.

HARVESTING GREEN GOLD

Getting the logs out is not such a problem. In the old days, they were simply "skidded" out of the woods by teams of horses. Men used axes to chop down the trees. Today, the harvesting is automated. Power saws cut the forest silence and huge machines lift the logs onto trucks that carry the wood overland to a port or to market. In fact, many of the roads in Finland were built to accommodate the transport of wood from the interior to the ships in the harbors. The country's rivers are still used as watery highways for floating logs to the sawmills and harbors. That's a cheap and easy way of getting a lot of wood to market.

But it takes a lot of muscle to be a logger, even with all that modern equipment. Brave lumberjacks still leap across logs drifting downstream. They still use long poles to break up jams.

Machines lift logs onto a truck for transportation to a port or market.

They still need to be careful when those tall pines come crashing to the ground. It is a tough, exciting, and dangerous job.

The Central Association of Finnish Forest Industries now oversees the various forestry companies. The association was founded in 1918 to promote commercial and industrial uses of wood. It represents the forest industry on government committees and in trade negotiations with other countries, and carries out research work and many related operations. The association even has its own press, the Finnish Paper and Timber Journal Publishing Company, which prints three magazines and a directory of the forest industry.

Looking after the companies' interests in the forests is the responsibility of the Employers' Association of Finnish Forest Industries, a separate organization.

Smoke from the Rautaruukki Oy steel factory rises over the wooden houses of Raahe.

OTHER INDUSTRY

Many other industries contribute to Finland's economic well-being. Factories are concentrated in the southern third of the country; most have head offices in Helsinki. Several groups oversee the workings of all these companies: the Confederation of Finnish Industries, the Finnish Foreign Trade Association, and Finnfacts Institute.

The metal and engineering industry employs more than 180,000 people, about 35 percent of the total work force in Finland. The Finns are great at building machines and ships—which you might say is a spin-off or at least a complementary business to forestry. The machines are used to harvest the timber, and the ships are used to transport it to foreign ports. Finland is also one of Europe's leading producers of cranes and lifts, many of which are used in forestry work. Some look like giant monsters and can lift tons of logs at one time.

The Finns are experts at making stainless steel; steel plate, tubes, wire, and bars; and copper tubes. This so-called basic metal industry is one of the fastest expanding parts of the Finnish economy. The country exports tons of finished metal goods each year. They are snapped up by other industrialized nations that use the materials in their own products.

A number of plants also are now making electrical motors, generators, and transformers. Some of the gear is used in factories and some for train engines, on ships, and in tractors. The Finns make top-quality radio and television equipment, as well as electronic devices for use in hospitals and in the mining industry. Printing, plastics, and chemicals are other growing Finnish markets.

Shipbuilding at the Wärtsilä docks

The country's love of the sea has meant that there always was a strong shipbuilding industry. All that wood was a natural raw material for constructing sailing ships. Skilled craft workers and carpenters contributed to the Finnish economy hundreds of years ago. Even English customers placed orders for vessels. Ostrobothnia, on the eastern shore of the Gulf of Bothnia, was the shipbuilding capital of the world in the 1700s.

The advent of steamships boosted the Finnish shipbuilding industry. Everyone recognized the high quality of the ships made by the Finns. Finnish shipping became an important livelihood for many people. Even with the appearance of steel steamers, many Finns clung to their wooden-hulled vessels. Old sailors fondly remembered the days of the great "wheat races" between shipowners whose vessels carried cargo from Australia to Great Britain. The record is held by the four-masted barque *Parma*, which sailed from Victoria, Australia to Falmouth, England, in eighty-three days in 1933.

Icebreakers like this one help keep Finland's seaports open during the winter.

For years, though, winters clogged the northern ports with ice. Ships were locked in until the spring thaw. But in 1890, Finland commissioned its first icebreaker, the *Murtaja* (which means "Breaker"). The first time that ship smashed the ice jams outside the Finnish ports, the sailors cheered. They would finally be able to get some work done in winter. The *Murtaja* was retired in 1958, after a long and honorable career.

The Finland Steamship Company played a crucial role in the development of winter navigation and the maritime future of the country. It was the first to build ships specifically reinforced for crunching through the ice. They had thicker and stronger metal hulls, more-closely spaced ribs, and engines considerably more powerful than did ordinary vessels of the same size. The icebreakers could smash through the thickest ice, leading convoys of cargo ships to ports to the south and west.

As were many other countries, Finland was hard hit by the Great Depression of the 1930s, when banks and businesses lost

A Silja Line cruise ship

money and closed their doors. The Finnish shipping industry was socked just as hard, but some shrewd business people still were able to save enough money to buy ships at rock-bottom prices. When the depression finally ended, the shipping companies were able to recover—but not for long. Along came World War II, which put an end to shipping for several years. There were too many submarines, torpedoing anything that moved across the seas.

In addition, when Finland and the Soviet Union signed their peace treaty in 1944, Finland had to surrender 104 merchant ships to the Russians as part of the war reparations. That really hurt. But after the war, the industry slowly recovered. The Finnish merchant fleet now numbers about 450 ships. It even has some huge oil tankers on the oceans today.

The Finns consider short-distance hauling just as important. A number of car and train ferries, as well as merchant vessels, sail between Scandinavian ports or to Germany. The Viking Line and the Silja ("Seal") Line are among the biggest. They make most of their runs to Sweden.

Most farms in Finland are small and privately owned.

In one recent year, the two firms carried 3.5 million passengers, 427,000 cars, 28,700 buses, and 105,000 units of cargo. The largest ferryboats each can transport 2,000 passengers, several hundred passenger cars, and several dozen trucks.

Finland's reputation as a tourist attraction draws many of these passengers, who also enjoy puttering around on the inland lakes. The Finns have built many cruise ships to service the vacationers. The ships connect with highways and rail lines, making it easy for foreigners to see much of Finland's scenery.

The country's biggest shipyards are in Turku and Helsinki. They sell to many different nations. Even Argentina ordered an icebreaker for use in Antarctica. In addition to making ships, Finnish firms also make motors, fittings, compasses, and other related items.

FOOD, TEXTILES, AND FURS

Finnish farm products are highly regarded. The country has traditionally considered itself a society that is basically agricultural. Of course, it isn't quite that way anymore because of

On clear days, Finns wash their handmade rugs in seawater and hang them out to dry on long racks.

the growth of the timber and shipbuilding industries. But the Finns have a love of the land handed down from those long generations that were self-sufficient in a rugged environment. More Finns live in cities than on farms. But whenever possible, city dwellers plant an urban garden.

The food industry today is basically geared toward exports. Cheese, milk powder, meat products, chocolates, refined sugar, butter, breads, and liqueurs are top sellers abroad. But the best-selling export by far is Finnish vodka, a strong alcoholic drink. More than five million liters (1,320,860 gallons) a year are sold to foreign markets.

Anyone who designs or makes clothes or home furnishings is probably familiar with Finnish textiles. The Finns are famous for their ladies' dresses, men's suits, ski clothing, interior decoration textiles, and similar woven fabrics. Colorful *rya* rugs decorate many Finnish homes. On clear days, Finns wash their rugs outside and hang them to dry on long racks. Tradition says that water from the Baltic Sea is especially good for keeping the brilliant hues in the rugs.

Finland is also the world's largest exporter of furs. Mink and blue fox are raised on large breeding farms; their skins are used in the clothing industry almost everywhere.

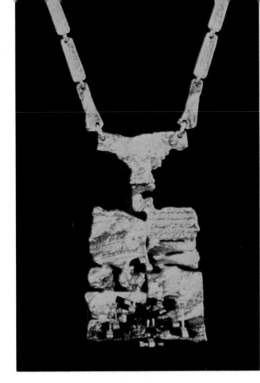

Finnish designers are famous the world over for their jewelry, furniture, glassware, ceramics, and cutlery.

Five times a year in Copenhagen, Denmark, Finnish traders participate in the international fur auctions that attract buyers from the United States, France, Spain, Canada, Italy, West Germany, and Great Britain.

The country is also a leader in the design of furniture, glassware, jewelry, handicrafts, footwear, leather products, ceramics, and cutlery. A number of associations keep watch over these industries; many sponsor art exhibits, craft shows, and museum displays of their respective specialties. The Museum of Applied Arts, the Finnish Society of Crafts and Design, the Association of Finnish Designers Ornamo, Oy Finnish Design Center AB, the Finnish Furniture Exporters' Association, the Finnish Glass and Ceramics Manufacturers' Association, and the Finnish Goldsmiths' Association are only a few of the groups that make sure quality is maintained.

The world knows that it can count on the quality of these and the rest of Finnish goods. That's why Finnish industry has so many repeat customers!

A famous summer opera festival is held in the courtyard
of Olavinlinna Castle at Savonlinna (above). The Pori Jazz
Festival (below) attracts music lovers from all over.

Chapter 7

A MECCA FOR MUSIC
AND THE ARTS

There must be something in the Finnish air that makes such beautiful music pour from the hearts of the people. They seem to be swept up with sound, whether it be soaring classical music or pop and rock. Music is an integral part of Finnish society. It's impossible for anyone to spend much time in Finland without being urged to attend a concert. The country has at least nine internationally renowned music festivals that draw eager listeners from around the world. You are in excellent company whether attending the organ music fest in Lahti; the chamber festivals in Turku, Jyväskylä, or Kumo; the Pori Jazz Festival; folk dancing and music at Kuopio or Kaustinen; the grand opera at Savonlinna; or classical, pop, or rock fests in Helsinki.

It makes no difference to a Finn if a favorite musician is performing at Helsinki's Finlandia Hall or in a grassy field. It's the music that matters.

Many Finns have well-stocked musical libraries at home. Finnlevy is an internationally recognized album producer, specializing in classics. Other recording companies also lend their talents to the music field.

A long winter night often is passed by curling up in a chair and listening to a recording of Seppo Laamanen on the cello and Timo Mikkila on the piano. Other music lovers might prefer an American jazz artist or a Latin American band. Talking about music is a favorite pastime for Finns, especially right after listening to a recording or a live performance.

The Finns have the best of two worlds. They love showing off their great talented performers, especially at the Helsinki Festival. This allows foreign visitors to get a sampling of the Finnish musical heritage and culture. On the other hand, overseas performers have the chance to play before Finnish audiences. Because Finland is so close to the Soviet Union, many Soviet performers come to present concerts and recitals. Finland has hosted Russian superstars but has also cordially offered stage room for lesser-known performers.

The Finns are very aware of their own heritage. This has helped them to survive as a people under so many different rulers. Perhaps because they made it through those difficult times, they have learned to appreciate the culture of other nations. The Finns are open to all sorts of musical styles, from accordion music to Orthodox church chorus music.

During the summer, Finland is home to some seventy youth music camps. Courses last from two to three weeks, and there are always long lists of students waiting to enroll. During the Finnish summer, the music seems to stop for only two or three hours a day, when the sun briefly disappears. The Finns call this musical explosion "the pleasant madness."

There are eleven symphony orchestras in Finland and six

The stunning Sibelius monument in Helsinki was designed by Eila Hiltunen, one of Finland's most gifted sculptors.

smaller professional town orchestras. The largest—the Helsinki Philharmonic, the Radio Symphony, and the Orchestra of the Finnish National Opera—are located in Helsinki. The finances and operations of these orchestras are secure. Many of the musicians are on the city payroll and receive aid from the central government.

It has been said that "along with paper and wood, Finnish opera singers are the most sought-after export." At least twenty-five Finnish opera singers are working abroad. The celebrated bassos Kim Borg and Matti Lehtinen were among the first to carry the Finnish musical torch afield. They first worked out of the country in the 1950s. Then there were Martti Talvela, Matti Salminen, Tom Krause, Jorma Hynninen, and Walton Grönroos. Female singers also have been well received. Taru Valjakka and Irma Urrila are among the most noteworthy.

Famous composers over the years have included Bernhard Henrik Crusell (1775-1838) and Jean Sibelius (1865-1957). Their

Finnish folk musicians play at a summer festival.

compositions drew heavily on the country's folk music heritage. More modern composers, such as Uuno Klami and Aarre Merikanto, incorporate new themes into some of their music, but they love and appreciate the traditional melodies.

Folk music is very important for the Finns. Their country is a meeting point for eastern and western sounds. The cultural influences on Finnish music range from English ballads to Slavic dances. Songs of many kinds, originally sung by animal herders, were the beginnings of Finnish folk music. The fiddle became very important in the seventeeth century, a period of heavy Swedish influence. Soon, along came the accordion—a relatively easy instrument to play—and it caught on swiftly. A beloved dance, the polka, made its way to Finland from another country. It started in Poland, moved to Sweden, and eventually edged its way into Finland.

Of all the musical styles incorporated into Finnish music, jazz alone has been reworked and given back to the world. Finnish jazz musicians have kept up with the times; many perform and study in the United States and Europe. They include saxophonist Eero Koivistoinen and guitarists Jukka Tolonen and Pekka Pohjola. Pianist Heikki Sarmanto also writes his own compositions and has won numerous international awards. His biggest success was "The New Hop Jazz Mass," which was premiered in St. Peter's Church in New York City in 1978. It also has been performed at the Newport Jazz Festival.

THEATER

Finns also enjoy the theater. There are some thirty-three professional companies in the country, four of which give performances in Swedish. Most receive public funds, including the Ylioppilasteatteri (the Student Theater) in Helsinki. Several plays usually run at the same time, performed by a resident company.

Finnish theaters come in a variety of sizes. The Finnish National Theater has three halls available for programs, ranging from 115 seats to 912. The tiny Teatteri Jurkka in Helsinki has only 50 seats.

The Finnish theater season runs from September to May; most of the professional theaters shut down in the summer, when the scene shifts to open-air stages. The most famous of these is Tampere's unusual Pyynikki Theater. Its stage runs around the outside of the eight-hundred-seat auditorium, which revolves so that the entire audience can see what is going on. Nobody seems to get dizzy. Most of the plays are by Finnish authors, yet there is a great deal of interest in foreign productions. England's Shakespeare remains a favorite.

READING AND WRITING

Finns are avid readers and enjoy authors from around the world. Books are expensive, however, so Finns flock to their three thousand or so libraries to find reading materials. Many of the university libraries also make their collections available to the public.

Not many Finnish authors are known in other countries, although the works of F. E. Sillanpää have been translated into twenty-four languages. Sillanpää won the Nobel Prize in literature in 1939. It wasn't until the Reformation of the late Middle Ages that Finns had much of a written language. Most of their folk tales were told aloud. But the Church supported the movement to teach reading, which meant that the Finns finally got to work putting their stories on paper. For a time, people who couldn't read were not allowed to be married. Of course, that gave a great boost to reading programs. Everybody was willing to learn to read after that law was passed!

An English ship captain who visited Finland in the 1850s said he was surprised that the Finns could read so well. He admitted that he always had thought they were rather backward and uneducated. The Finns, in turn, were surprised that so many English were illiterate—that they couldn't read or write.

Recent Finnish writers include Mika Waltari, who wrote many historical romances, and Väinö Linna, who is famous for his novel *The Unknown Soldier*, set during the Continuation War.

Finns enjoy reading newspapers and magazines; nearly every town in the country has its own morning paper. Most are in Finnish, but at least seven are in Swedish. A majority of the papers are owned by political parties. But Finland's largest, the

Old structures from all over Finland have been brought together on Seurasaari Island in Helsinki to form an outdoor folk museum.

Helsingin Sanomat in Helsinki, is independent. In addition to newspapers, there are about fifteen hundred different magazines in Finland, ranging from sports publications to those dealing with news and current events.

MUSEUMS

Finland likes to keep in touch with its past, basically through its museums. The impressive National Museum is in Helsinki. It traces the history of Finland from early days to the present. The Helsinki City Museum, the Zoological Museum, the Railway Museum, and the Atheneum Art Gallery are very well respected in the capital. One of the most unusual places is the Seurasaari, an outdoor facility in Helsinki where houses and buildings from all over Finland have been brought together. They were all rebuilt on an island, accessible by ferryboat, a few miles from the city center.

Outlying cities such as Turku also have numerous museums. Uusikaupunki on the west coast has a collection of windmills, while at Mariehamn on the Åland Islands there is a very fine museum containing relics from sailing days.

*Folk dancers in national costumes perform
during one of Finland's many summer festivals.*

NATIONAL COSTUMES

Finnish young people are surrounded by their heritage through their music and crafts. Every holiday calls for a fiddle tune, a dance, or a church service. So every holiday naturally means dressing up—frequently in national costumes.

Extra-special clothes are worn on Midsummer Eve, the Friday closest to June 24. Houses are decorated with birch tree branches, twigs, and flowers for this celebration of spring and summer. For traditional holidays such as Christmas, Easter, and Finnish Independence Day (December 6), mothers and fathers brush off costumes and air them out, to be ready for church, school, or government programs.

Weddings and other family occasions also bring out the dress-up costumes for boys and girls. Outfits run from $150 to $600, depending on how fancy they are. Most are handmade; each of the twelve provinces of Finland has a slightly different style. The girls' and women's outfits consist of wide, full skirts that can be striped or of a solid color and laced sleeveless vests of a matching or contrasting design. Unmarried girls wear colored ribbons in their hair, while married women wear small caps. Boys' and men's costumes are generally made up of long trousers and vests with wide lapels and narrow, stand-up collars, as well as full-sleeved shirts and skull caps. In some parts of Finland, the men wear very tight pants that hug the legs. Everyone loves to dance. It's a pleasure to see the floor fill up with twirling, swirling costumes. It's that music again.

The old and new ways of doing things mix well in Finland. Helsinki must be the disco capital of Europe; dance halls there stay open—and very lively—almost all night long.

EDUCATION

Finnish young people have to attend school from the age of seven to sixteen. Education is usually free. Local governments provide free meals, textbooks, health care, and transportation, if necessary.

About 30 percent of the Finnish population is under twenty-five. The government was very concerned about teaching all those young people, so it revised the educational system in the late 1960s. Youngsters go to a "comprehensive" school called the *peruskoulu*. They take standard classes, with lots of work in math, science, reading skills, history, and social studies—much as in other countries. At sixteen, the young people can either leave school and go to work or continue on to the *lukio*, which is a senior secondary school. That helps them get ready for university training.

In the old days, students were called *ylioppilas*, a term that came from *ylioppilastutkinto*, a general test that everyone had to pass before being allowed to go to advanced schools. That old tradition

*Since about 30 percent of the Finnish population is
under twenty-five, visitors to Finland sometimes get
the impression that they're surrounded by young people.*

of test taking will probably die out as the new educational system takes hold across the country.

The first university in Finland was founded in 1640 by the Swedes in Turku. It was moved to Helsinki in 1828, after a fire destroyed most of Turku. Today, the University of Helsinki is bilingual; students speak both Swedish and Finnish. Now there are also other universities around the country. But they aren't the only form of higher education in Finland. Currently, *korkeakoulu* (colleges) offer degrees, as do technical, nursing, business, theology, music, and economics schools.

Students at the university level attend many lectures and are faced with hours of homework. Often the students complain that they can't spend enough time with individual professors and don't receive the guidance they need. A great number of Finnish students are married shortly after enrolling in the universities. They go to work at jobs outside of school, which means that many don't become as involved in on-campus activities as do students in other countries.

Finnish universities have only two terms, one in the fall and another in the spring. However, there are summer courses for those who wish to cram a lot of learning into four or five weeks.

University seniors take part in school administration as members of school councils. They help decide school rules and assist with disciplinary problems. All university students belong to self-governing student corporations that offer cultural and social services.

Finnish schools try to prepare students for the work world. It also is hoped they will be touched by the arts in many ways that they can carry with them over the years following graduation. It's a big task.

These hardy Finnish skiers welcome the winter snows.

Chapter 8

LIFE-STYLES, HEROES, AND REINDEER

Young people in Finland are much like those in any other country. They enjoy bicycle riding, camping, sports, and dancing. They haven't had an easy life recently; a worldwide economic slump has resulted in much unemployment. But people are not generally discouraged.

The Finns always seem to be hanging on the brink of economic disaster. They grumble a lot about high prices, high taxes, and low wages. Political scientists shake their heads when they look at the Finnish way of doing things. Outsiders often have a hard time understanding the country's tendency to live it up today and worry about tomorrow only when tomorrow comes.

The country's financial difficulties are tied into the international scheme of things. The Finns must import crude oil; if other nations don't buy a lot of their products, the Finnish economy suffers no matter how expertly Finnish goods are produced.

SOCIAL WELFARE

Though the government of Finland has many welfare programs, the services are not nearly as extensive as those provided by other Scandinavian countries.

Pregnant women, mothers, and children are entitled to free health care; families are given a yearly allowance for each child under the age of sixteen; students in public elementary schools receive free books, medical and dental care, and one meal a day; and all Finns are covered by health insurance.

Contributions toward these welfare services are deducted from the paychecks of Finnish workers. When unemployment is high, the burden is heavier on those who are working. Yet Finns are usually cheerful in spite of what happens. They have been through so much over the centuries that few things really bother them anymore. They are happy to help each other out, whether in building a home or planning a sports club. That neighborly spirit pervades the national soul, assisting everyone in getting over the hump—whether it is an economic crisis, war, or whatever.

WOMEN'S ROLE

The Finns are open-minded about many things, especially in the area of women's rights. Women are more than stay-at-homes. Finnish women were the first in Europe permitted to vote in national elections. Under the law, husbands and wives are equal. Many university professors are women. There are women in parliament, at the head of political parties, and in the top ranks of industry. Recently, a woman police officer was Finland's representative to Interpol, the international police organization.

Probably a third of all jobs in Finland are held by women; they work in the sawmills, as truck drivers, and as construction laborers. Women performers and artists, such as sculptor Eila Hiltunen, are highly respected.

When it comes to dating, Finnish girls are just as likely to ask a boy for a date as vice versa. Women have a keen sense of their own worth in Finland.

YOUNG PEOPLE

The Finns really care about their young people. They don't like to see them unemployed.

Youth work comes under the direction of the Finnish Ministry of Education. In 1945, the government recommended that each commune set up a board to help young people secure jobs, in addition to providing sports and social outlets. Young men and women are appointed to positions on these boards and help recommend programs and activities. The government also supports youth camps, student centers, and activity areas for young people.

Political organizations, schools, parishes, and religious groups also organize programs and direct a lot of youth work .

Young people in Finland are very concerned about international matters. Finnish youth organizations have been strongly supportive of the peace and antinuclear war movements. They planned and ran the World Forum of Youth and Students for Peace, Detente, and Disarmament in Finland in 1981. They also have participated in many other programs promoting international cooperation. Finland has a State Youth Council, which helps Finnish youth groups work with those in other

Linnanmäki Amusement Park in Helsinki

countries. Meetings, seminars, camps, and cultural exchanges are popular. On the local level, Finnish communes have promoted the "twin town" concept, in which young people exchange visits with youths in cities overseas.

The concern the Finns have for their young people is obvious to anyone who visits Linnanmäki Amusement Park in Helsinki. The bright lights and sounds from the park, one of the largest in Europe, spill over the capital city from high on Castle Hill.

The history of the park goes back to the mid-1940s, when one of Finland's major problems was caring for its thousands of war orphans. In 1945, six children's charities joined forces to promote a lottery; the money collected was to be distributed among the organizing groups. To help attract crowds, carnival rides were rented. By 1950, the success of the lottery and the carnival led to the idea of building an amusement park. All the profits would go to an umbrella Children's Foundation, a major charity. And so Linnanmäki was built.

Most Finnish shoppers prefer selecting their fish and produce at the outdoor markets that can be found in nearly every city, town, and village.

The park is open from the end of April to the end of September. Everyone in Finland seems to visit Linnanmäki at least a couple of times a year, just to ride the giant wooden roller coaster, watch the shows, play the arcade games, and eat, eat, eat.

FOOD

Speaking of eating, that's one of the Finns' most enduring pastimes. The emphasis is on quantity, joke all the cooks. The *nakkimakkara* is a close relative of the hot dog; other sausages are the *berliinimakkara* and *teemakkara*. Reindeer sausage is called *poromakkara*. Meatballs also are popular, as are fish and french fried potatoes—similar to the English fish-and-chips.

Spicy minced meat rolled in cabbage leaves is delicious. So is *karjalanpaisti*, a stew made from pork, veal, and mutton. Homemade soup is a popular dish in Finland; pea soup (*hernekeitto*) is a traditional menu item for Thursday lunches.

Crayfish are a favorite Finnish summer delicacy.

On Christmas, the holiday meal would not be complete without boiled cod. This is followed by *riisipuro*, a dish that tastes like unsweetened rice pudding. An almond is hidden in one of the servings; tradition says that whoever finds it will be married that year. Nobody says what happens if the lucky finder is already married!

During the summer, boiled crayfish are eaten in great quantities. Catching the swift little creatures is often a family affair, a good excuse for a weekend away from the city.

Finns are almost addicted to milk products. They like cream in their coffee and also enjoy various types of sour milk, such as *piimä, kefiiri, viili,* and regular yogurt. Few people in Finland drink tea; most adults are coffee drinkers. Supposedly, they drink more than nine times as much coffee as do people who live in England. The coffee break is a habit everywhere.

Finnish people don't eat large breakfasts, but usually have only coffee and a *pulla*, a sweet, breadlike bun. Lunch (*lounas*), consisting of soup and a sandwich, is usually eaten in the late morning. Even businesspeople seldom bother with big noonday

A typical Finnish voileipäpöytä *(smorgasbord)*

meals. Youngsters get school lunches. Menus are published in the daily papers, so the children can groan ahead of time about the cafeteria meals. Dinner (*päivällinen*) is served between five and six o'clock. It often consists of a beef dish or fish, followed by a rich dessert, more coffee, and a glass of milk.

Restaurants tend to be expensive in Finland. Many of them offer *voileipäpöytä*, which is the Finnish version of a smorgasbord. They usually have three separate long tables that are laden with food. First, there's the cold table, with salads and sandwich meats. Next comes the hot table, with the main courses. And finally, there is the sweets table. This table is always full of cake, pies, and candies—usually with lots of chocolate.

Every restaurant and coffeehouse door is watched over by a porter, called the *vahtimestari*, whose job it is to check over the customers. Men without neckties are not admitted to many of the fancier places, but that custom is gradually being relaxed. Guests are supposed to tip the porter when they leave. Anyone who doesn't gets a dirty look.

SPORTS

Working off all that food is no problem, even in the winter, when some persons might prefer to stay inside and gain weight. The Finn heads for the open country with cross-country skis, skates, or a sled. For these hardy northern folk, a snowdrift is nothing more than one more challenge to overcome.

Olympic and world-champion skiers from Finland include Veli Saarinen, Veikko Hakulinen, Eero Mäntyranta, and Helena Takalo. All the young people look up to ski-jumping champs Antti Hyvärinen and Veikko Kankkonen. Back in the 1920s, Finns admired their world-champion speed skater Clas Thunberg, who rolled up Olympic points with ease. Kaija Mustonen, a female speed skater, brought an Olympic gold medal home to Finland in 1968.

Rowing, running, and wrestling are the most popular sports in Finland, followed closely by archery, bowling, and Finnish baseball, called *pesäpallo.* Organized team sports started in Finland as early as the 1870s; the country captured a gold medal in wrestling during the 1906 Olympics.

Finland has always been a land of long-distance runners; the most notable was Paavo Nurmi, the "Flying Finn." Nurmi has been considered one of the greatest sportsmen of all time. Between 1920 and 1932, he set twenty world track records and won nine Olympic gold medals as an individual runner, in addition to capturing other gold medals in team competition.

Finns take a keen interest in keeping fit. That's why they ski so much and enjoy other vigorous outings. There are numerous sports organizations in Finland; international activities are coordinated by the Finnish Central Sports Federation. Another

Finns enjoy all kinds of sports, including winter
kick-sled races (above) and foot races and hiking (below).

Many visitors to Finland take advantage of hotel saunas such as this one.

major sports group is the Workers' Sports Federation. The government-sponsored soccer pool pumps a lot of money into the various sporting associations. Many Finns like to gamble on soccer teams each weekend, knowing their money goes to a good cause.

THE SAUNA

Even if some Finns don't care to jump, run, or tumble, no one ignores the sauna. Finns appreciate life's simpler pleasures: the first hand-picked strawberries of the season; the year's first snowfall, with its thick wet flakes; the delicious taste of salted herring and spring potatoes; and the sauna.

For the Finn, a sauna routine is more than a beauty treatment. It meets a practical need: cleaning up after a hard day's work. In the old days, a Finn always built his sauna before he built his home. A long day of chopping wood ended on a pleasant note by the

"Polar Bear" swimming is part of a typical Finnish sauna routine.

fireside, encased in steam. Hotel saunas are okay, but there's nothing to match bathing alongside a lake, with a fresh birch twig to scrape the skin and keep the blood singing.

The *saunamakkara*, a sausage grilled on the sauna stove, is a delicious treat afterward, especially when smothered with mustard and downed with beer to help adults cool off. Pronounce *sauna* as if it were written "sow-na." If you can do that, you are well on your way to making firm Finnish friends.

HOLIDAYS

Finns thoroughly enjoy their public holidays and vacations, when they are able to take time off from work and head for their

On Midsummer Eve, bonfires flare on lakes all over Finland.

vacation homes. In addition to an annual vacation, which usually lasts about four weeks, the Finns also have free days on January 1, Good Friday, Easter Monday, May 1 (*Vappu,* which marks the coming of spring), Midsummer (*Juhannus,* on the nearest Saturday to June 24), All Saints' Day, Independence Day (December 6), and Christmas. On New Year's Eve, youngsters try to tell their fortunes by pouring melted lead into a bucket of cold water, where it hardens again. The various shapes are supposed to indicate what the future will bring.

The holidays are equally divided between religious and secular occasions. Probably 95 percent of the Finns belong to some church, but that doesn't mean they are churchgoers. Actually, only a few attend services each Sunday; most Finns seem to prefer puttering around their homes or being outdoors at that time.

Kerimaki (left) is one of the largest wooden churches in the world. On the right is the imposing Lutheran Cathedral in Helsinki.

The largest of the churches is the Evangelical Lutheran Church; its membership is more than 4.5 million—this is about 93 percent of the population. Next comes the Orthodox Church of Finland, with sixty thousand members. There are only a few Roman Catholic parishes. Jehovah's Witnesses, Finnish Free Church members, Jews, and Muslims round out the church population.

Both the Lutheran and Orthodox churches are state churches. Each parish is allowed to levy a tax on members within its area. Remember the old law that said people couldn't be married if they couldn't read? There is still a law on the books that states officially that no one can wed if he or she hasn't paid the church tax!

This Lapp family is dressed in colorful national costumes.

THE LAPPS

The Lapps, most of whom live in the far north, were originally pagans but were converted to Christianity. Unfortunately, the missionaries destroyed the drums the Lapps used to use in their rites and outlawed many of their rituals. Many young Lapps today are returning to some of the old traditions in an attempt to keep their heritage alive.

Civilization, or at least the encroachment of industry and the establishment of national borders, has put a crimp in the nomadic life of the Lapps. Many now have settled in villages and towns and look for work there. Finland has a Commission on Lapp Affairs to help Lapps adjust to their new way of life. Reindeer herding is not as widespread as it used to be, but it still plays an important role in the lives of many Lapp families. The animals are allowed to graze on the pastures of northern Norway, Sweden, and Finland in the summer months.

Building a Lapp tent

During September and October, the reindeer are herded into corrals to be sorted and counted. The autumn roundup is an exciting time for Lapps. It's the chance to talk about the past year and get caught up on friends' activities.

The reindeer's basic food is lichen, which is a mossy growth covering rocks. When lichen is covered with snow, the reindeer can dig it out with hooves that are shaped like shovels. In the spring, the reindeer are moved back out to the lowland pastures until summer's warmth and the nasty Finnish mosquitoes mean that it's time to migrate farther north.

In earlier years, the Lapps obtained meat, milk, leather, and skins from their reindeer. The reindeer also were used as pack animals and for pulling sleighs. Most of today's Lapps use snowmobiles, however, rather than depending on their four-legged charges.

Not all Lapps herded reindeer over the years. The River Lapps were basically fishermen, the Forest Lapps were hunters, and the

*These Lapps
are preparing
a cooking
fire for their
midday meal.*

Coast Lapps were sailors and fishermen. Each area has its own
dialect, and Lapps often have difficulty communicating if they are
not neighbors. They often have to speak Finnish or Swedish to be
understood by each other—which adds to the already complicated
language situation in Finland. The Lapps have their own
newspapers. Unlike the spoken dialects, the written word can be
understood by all Lapps. There are regional radio and television
programs for them as well.

The future of the Lapps as a separate minority is unclear. They
are gradually being absorbed into the mainstream of Finnish life,
yet their culture will probably not disappear entirely. They, like
all Finns, are tied too closely to the countryside to fade away
altogether.

The Finns dream of an idyllic, woodsy form of life—the way it was centuries ago. They can be very moody and quiet, much like their deep forests. Confronted with today's rush and all the resulting pressures, the Finns sometimes simply want to put today aside and return to the way they imagine things used to be. This isn't to say they aren't forward looking or eager for new challenges. They certainly are. Yet they always carry an inner feeling that somewhere there is a place for reflection, a place for regrouping thoughts, a place where nature and spirit can come together.

This is Finland's enchantment.

An asterisk (*) refers to the approximate location of a place that does not appear on the map.

Norway, Sweden and Finland

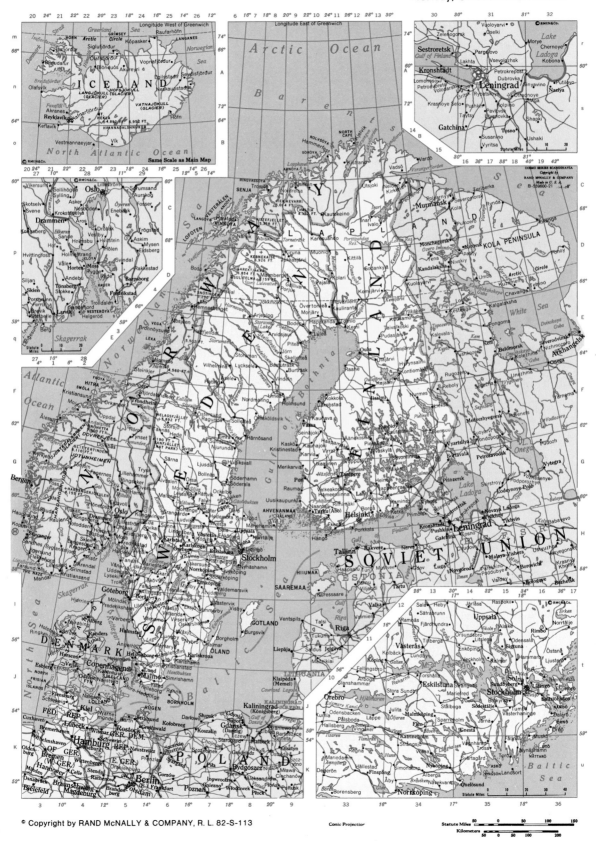

Conic Projection

MINI-FACTS AT A GLANCE

GENERAL INFORMATION

Official Name: Republic of Finland (*Suomi* in Finnish)

Capital: Helsinki

Official Languages: Finnish and Swedish

Other Languages: Lapps speak their own language.

Government: Finland is a republic. The president is the head of state. The president handles foreign relations and is commander in chief of the armed forces. After the president, the most important government figure is the prime minister, who is head of the government and the Council of State. The one-house parliament (the *Eduskunta*) consists of two hundred representatives who are elected by the people for four-year terms. All citizens over the age of eighteen may vote. Finland is divided into twelve provinces, each headed by a governor appointed by the national president. Local government functions are carried out by communes, each with a council elected by the people. The present government is based on the constitution of 1919.

Flag: The national flag has a blue cross on a white field, representing the blue waters and white snows of Finland.

Coat of Arms: The coat of arms features a golden lion on a red field. The lion is brandishing a silver sword in an armored paw. Its hind legs are trampling a silver scimitar, which is a long, curved sword. The lion is wearing a crown and is surrounded by nine silver roses—symbols of the traditional provinces of Finland. This coat of arms was first used on the tomb of King Gustavus Vasa of Sweden (1523-1560) when Finland was still a part of the Swedish kingdom. The standard was kept even when Finland was a grand duchy of Russia (1809-1917).

National Song: "Our Land," with words by J.L. Runeberg and music by Fredrik Pacius; in Finnish it is called *"Maamme;"* in Swedish, *"Vårt Land."*

Religion: About 97 percent of the population belongs to the Evangelical Lutheran Church.

Money: Money in Finland is measured in marks. The Finnish mark is divided into 100 pennies. There are coins of 5, 10, 20, and 50 pennies, 1 mark, and 5 marks. The notes (paper money) are worth 1 mark, 5, 10, 50, 100, and 500 marks. In October, 1990, one United States dollar was worth approximately 3.68 marks.

Weights and Measures: Finland uses the metric system.

Population: 4,978,000 (1990 estimate)

Cities: Over half of the people in Finland live in cities.

Helsinki 490,693
Tampere 171,608
Turku 159,346
Espoo 169,587
Vantaa 152,573
Lahti . . . . no estimate
Oulu . . . . no estimate

(Population figures based on 1990 government estimates)

GEOGRAPHY

Highest Point: Mount Haltia, 4,357 ft. (1,328 m)

Lowest Point: Sea level

Coastline: Mapmakers say the coastline is 700 to 3,000 mi. (1,126 to 4,827 km).

Rivers: Longest river in Finland is the Kemijoki, 340 mi. (547 km).

Lakes: Lake Saimaa is the largest lake, 680 square mi. (1,760 km²); it is located in the southeast part of the lake region in central Finland.

Mountains: There are a few mountainous areas in the northwest adjacent to the borders with Sweden and Norway.

Climate: Finland lies in the snow and forest zone characterized by cold, damp winters and warm summers. Thanks to the North Atlantic Current and the prevailing winds, the mean temperatures are much higher at all times of the year than in other countries in the same latitude.

July temperatures average between 55° and 63° F. (13° and 17° C). The lowest winter temperature is below -22° F. (-30° C) and the mean temperature in February is 7° to 26° F. (-14° to -3° C). Because Finland lies so far north, the difference between the amount of sunlight in the summer and the winter is great. The longest day in the south is close to nineteen hours and the shortest six hours. In Lapland there is the greatest difference. In one section, for example, the sun in summer does not set for seventy-three days, but in the depths of winter, it doesn't rise for fifty-one days. During the long night, however, the aurora borealis (northern lights) can be seen.

Greatest Distances: North to south—720 mi. (1,159 km)
East to west—335 mi. (539 km)

Area: 130,094 sq. mi. (336,943 km²), including 12,206 sq. mi. (31,613 km²) of inland waters

The Lake District

NATURE

Trees: Common trees include oak, willow, maple, and alder, mostly in southern and central Finland. Pine, spruce, and birch are plentiful in the north. The lumber industry accounts for almost three quarters of Finland's exports. The country produces over 1.1 billion cu. ft. (30 million m^3) of timber per year.

Fish, ocean: Baltic herring, pike, salmon, sea trout

Fish, inland: Pike, perch, vendace, whitefish

Animals: There are sixty-seven species of wild mammals in Finland, including lynx, fox, muskrat, white-tailed deer, and beaver. Bears, wolves, and wolverines have decreased in numbers greatly in recent years. The beaver had been extinct, but was recently reintroduced. Elk are plentiful.

Birds: There are about 230 species of birds in Finland.

EVERYDAY LIFE

Food: The Finns especially like fish, sausage, beef, veal, pork, and boiled potatoes. Breakfast is usually light—some coffee and a *pulla*, a sweet, breadlike bun. Lunch, eaten in the late morning, usually consists of soup and a sandwich. The *nakkimakkara*, a relative of the hot dog; reindeer sausage, called *poromakkara;* meat balls; spicy stuffed cabbage; and soups of all kinds are common Finnish fare. The Finns are also very fond of milk products, and drink a great deal of coffee.

Holidays:

> January 1, New Year's Day
> Epiphany
> Good Friday
> Easter (two days)
> May 1 (May Day)
> Ascension Day
> Whitsun
> Midsummer Day (the nearest Saturday to June 24)
> All Saints' Day
> December 6 (Independence Day)
> December 25-26, (Christmas Day and Second Christmas Day)

Culture: Traditional Finnish folk culture has depended on influences from outside the country, particularly Sweden to the west and Russia to the east. But many of the country's greatest artistic achievements are homegrown. Witness the magnificent presentations of Jean Sibelius, the famous composer whose songs, tone poems, and seven symphonies have been praised around the world. Then there was novelist F.E. Sillanpää, who received the Nobel Prize in Literature in 1939. Notable architects were Eliel Saarinen and his son Eero, Alvar Aalto, and numerous others. Theater flourishes in Finland, as does opera, painting, and sculpture. Finnish design is famous around the world for textiles, ceramics, glass, jewelry, furniture, and light fixtures. There are also numerous museums in Finland, including a museum of windmills. Finns have a great interest in music. The country has at least nine internationally renowned music festivals. There are eleven symphony orchestras in Finland and six smaller professional town orchestras. Theater is also very popular. There are thirty-three professional companies in Finland, four of which perform in Swedish. All Finns are literate, and many are widely read. Public libraries are well patronized.

Language: (Phonetic spelling; every letter is pronounced, the main stress always on the first syllable.)

> *Hyvää päivää:* Good day; *Kiitos:* Thank you; *Olkaa hyvä:* Please; *Anteeksi:* Pardon, excuse me; *Hyvästi:* Good-bye; *Näkemiin:* So long.

Sports and Recreation: Finns love outdoor sports such as skiing and speed skating. They can boast many Olympic champions in both sports. They also enjoy rowing, running, wrestling, archery, bowling, and Finnish baseball (*pesäpallo*). The sauna, a special Finnish bath, is a tradition that is refreshing and relaxing.

Communications: There are about 1,500 magazines in Finland, 103 daily newspapers (12 are printed in Swedish), and nearly 150 weekly newspapers. Some 100 magazines are intended for the general public. Finns spend less time reading newspapers than listening to the radio or watching television. On the average, Finns use mass media about five hours a day. Radio and television each account for two hours and newspapers for barely an hour. The state controls the Finnish Broadcasting Company. A commercial television company leases air time from the state-run company.

Transportation: Finland is served by its national airline—Finnair—and many other international carriers. Finland has more than forty airports. The sea is also important to Finland, which has several major harbors—most notably Turku and Helsinki. Finland has numerous car and passenger ferries that take people and freight to other countries. Its shipbuilding industry makes icebreakers to keep the sea-lanes open in winter. The long water routes that connect the country's lake system are used by barges, tugs, and steamers for hauling freight and passengers. The state railways are the country's major transportation undertaking; thousands of miles of track connect all parts of Finland. There are also thousands of miles of surfaced and unsurfaced roads in Finland. Most are concentrated in south and central Finland. There are about four million registered vehicles in the country. Most of them are private cars; the rest are buses and trucks.

Schools: Education in Finland has undergone a recent reform. A nine-year school program has been developed. Children must attend school from ages seven to sixteen. The comprehensive schools are divided into a six-year lower level, where instruction is the same for all youngsters, and a three-year upper level, where more specialized studies are encouraged. Everyone must learn to read and speak two foreign languages. The most popular language studies, in addition to Swedish and Finnish, include English, German, French, and Russian. Studies for the first language begin in third grade and those for the second in seventh grade. Local governments provide free meals, textbooks, health care, and transportation, if necessary. The oldest university in Finland, the University of Turku, was founded in 1640. It was the only university until the beginning of this century. It was transferred to Helsinki and its name was changed at the beginning of the nineteenth century. There are now universities in Helsinki, Turku, Jyväskylä, Oulu, and Tampere. Before advancing to a university at the age of eighteen, a student must pass a test. Programs at Finland's universities take from four to seven years to complete.

Health: Everyone living in Finland is entitled to health care. Two acts concerning free, or nearly free, health care are in force: the 1963 Health Insurance Act and the 1972 Public Health Act. The national insurance covers a portion of physicians' fees, tests and treatment, travel costs, and medicines; some medicines are free. A daily allowance is paid to anyone whose illness results in a loss of income.

Principal Products:
Agriculture: Cheese, milk powder, cattle, pigs, meat products, chocolates, refined sugar, butter, breads, grains, potatoes, liqueurs, and vodka, cut flowers
Manufacturing: Stainless steel; steel plate, tubes, wire, and bars; and copper tubes
Lumber industry: Wood paneling, pulp, newsprint, printing and writing papers, furniture, and building products
Textiles: Women's dresses, men's suits, ski clothing, interior decoration textiles, and rya rugs
Furs: Mink and blue fox, raised on large breeding farms

IMPORTANT DATES

1100s-1200s—Sweden gradually takes over all of Finland

1155 or 1157—Legendary date when King Erik of Sweden sends English-born Bishop Henry of Uppsala on a crusade to Finland to baptize the Finns

1229—Turku founded

1362—Finland becomes a Swedish province

1397—Kalmar Union unites Danes, Finns, Norwegians, and Swedes under a common crown

1435—Arboga assembly established, first *riksdag* (parliament) in Sweden's history

1523—Gustavus Vasa becomes first hereditary monarch

1548—Bishop of Turku, Michael Agricola, translates the Prayer Book and the New Testament into Finnish

1550—Helsinki founded by Swedish King Gustavus

1556—Finland made a grand duchy of Sweden

1618-1648—Thirty Years War

1640—University of Turku founded

1718-1773—Sweden's "Age of Freedom"

1720-1721—Finland partly and sometimes completely occupied by Russian troops

1741-1743—War between Russia and Sweden, resulting in cession of part of Finland to Russia

1779—Tampere founded

1788-1790—War between Russia and Sweden; no Finnish territory lost

1807—Tsar Alexander I of Russia and Napoleon I of France sign agreement giving Russia the right to annex Finland

1809—Russia annexes Finland and Åland Island

1812—Helsinki becomes capital

1835—Publication of *Kalevala*, Finnish national folk epic

1846—Runeberg's "Our Land" becomes Finnish national anthem

1863—Tsar Alexander II proclaims Finnish an official language of law and administration on an equal footing with Swedish

1904—Finnish civil servant shoots and kills the Russian governor

1905 — Peasant revolution in Russia

1905 — Six-day nationwide strike against the Russian government

1906 — Universal suffrage adopted; Finland becomes first European country to give women the vote

1917 — Finnish independence proclaimed on December 6

1918 — Finnish "Reds" and "Whites" fight a civil war

1918 — Finnish parliament elects Prince Friedrich Karl of Hesse as ruler

1919 — Republican constitution adopted and Kaarlo Juho Ståhlberg elected president

1920 — Finland signs peace treaty with Russia

1921 — League of Nations awards Åland Islands to Finland after quarrel with Sweden over the islands

1930 — Communist party banned

1939 — German-Soviet treaty

1939-1940 — Winter War

1941-1944 — Continuation War

1944 — Carl Gustav Mannerheim becomes president and a new government is formed

1946 — Policy of neutrality in international politics established

1948 — Treaty on Friendship, Cooperation, and Mutual Assistance between Finland and the Soviet Union

1952 — Finland finishes paying its war reparations to the Soviet Union

1952 — Olympics held in Helsinki

1955 — Finland joins the United Nations and the Nordic Council

1961 — Finland becomes a member of the European Free Trade Association (EFTA)

1973 — Finnish parliament extends President Urho Kekkonen's term to 1978; he was first elected in 1956

1975 — Finland hosts the Congress for Security and Cooperation in Europe

1981 — Urho Kekkonen retires from office of president

1982 — Mauno Koivisto takes office of president

1987 — In March elections, Conservative Party makes stunning gains over Social Democrats; position of Communist Party weakened

1988—United Nations General Assembly votes to accept Finland as a new nonpermanent member to the Security Council

1989—Foreign Minister Kalevi Sorsa is succeeded by Pertti Paasio following a dispute within the party; Mauno Koivisto continues as president; United Nations Environmental Program meets in Helsinki and adopts a declaration to end production of ozone-damaging chemicals by the year 2000

1991—Esko Aho forms a new four party government as Finland's youngest premier; Seppo Raty bests his previous mark and sets a world javelin record with a throw of 318 feet, 1 inch

IMPORTANT PEOPLE

Alvar Aalto (1898-1976), architect, designed town plan for Rovaniemi, master plan for Imatra, and plan for the Helsinki Centre

Väinö Aaltonen (1894-1966), pioneering sculptor, carved bust of Sibelius

Adolf Ivar Arwidsson (1791-1858), historian, poet, and Finnish nationlist

Kim Borg (1919-   ), bass singer and music professor

Bernard Henrik Crusell (1775-1838), composer

Johan Albert Ehrenström (1762-1847), architect; with C.L. Engel, rebuilt Helsinki in the early nineteenth century; drafted Helsinki town plan

Carl Ludvig Engel (1778-1840), German-born architect who with J.A. Ehrenström rebuilt Helsinki in the early nineteenth century; most important contribution was the design of the Senate Square

Erik IX (d. 1160), patron saint of Sweden, king from 1150 to 1160

Friedrich Karl of Hesse (1860-1940), ruler of Finland for a few weeks in 1918

Walton Grönroos, singer

Veikko Hakulinen, world-champion skier

Bishop Henry of Uppsala (d. 1156), sent by King Erik IX to baptize the Finns; patron saint of Finland

Heikki von Hertzen (1913-   ), lawyer; planned and built city of Tapiola

Jorma Hynninen (1941-   ), opera baritone

Antti Hyvärinen, ski-jumping champion

Veikko Kankkonen, ski-jumping champion

Urho Kekkonen (1900-   ), president of the republic, 1956-1981

Aleksis Kivi (1834-72), dramatist and poet

Uuno Klami (1900-1962), modern composer

Eero Koivistoinen, saxophonist

Tom Krause (1934-   ), baritone, has sung with West Berlin Opera and Paris Opera

Seppo Laamanen, cellist

Matti Lehtinen (1922-   ), baritone singer

Väinö Linna (1920-   ), author of *The Unknown Soldier*

Carl Gustav Mannerheim (1867-1951), president of the republic, 1944-46

Close-up of the Sibelius Monument in Helsinki

Eero Mäntyranta, world-champion skier

Aarre Merikanto (1893-1958), modern composer

Timo Mikkila (1912-   ), pianist

Kaija Mustonen, female skater, 1968 Olympic gold medal winner

Paavo Nurmi (1897-1973), long-distance runner, Olympic gold medal winner

Juho K. Paasikivi (1870-1956), president, 1946-56

Pekka Pohjola, guitarist

Henrik Gabriel Porthan (1729-1809), known as the Father of Finnish history

Johan Ludvig Runeberg (1804-77), poet, wrote the words to the Finnish national anthem

Veli Saarinen, champion skier

Matti Salminen, male opera singer

Heikki Sarmanto, pianist

Jean Sibelius (1865-1957), most famous Finnish composer, wrote *Finlandia*

F.E. Sillanpää (1888-1964), won Nobel Prize in literature in 1939

Johan Wilhelm Snellman (1806-81), philosopher and journalist

Kaarlo Juho Ståhlberg (1865-1952), first president of Finland

Helena Takalo, world-champion skier

Martti Talvela (1935-   ), international opera and concert singer, bass

Zacharias Topelius (1818-98), author of historical novels and a Finnish nationalist

Clas Thunberg, Olympic speed skater in the 1920s

Irma Urrila, female opera singer

Taru Valjakka (1938-   ), soprano; has sung on international opera and concert stages

Gustavus Vasa (1496-1560), made Finland a grand duchy of Sweden in 1556

Mika Waltari (1908-   ), historical novelist, author of *The Egyptian,* translated into twenty-five languages

RULERS OF FINLAND

Swedish Rulers	Reign
King Erik IX	1150-60
(The Folkung Dynasty) (1250-1371)	
Earl Birger (regent)	1250-66
Waldemar (king)	1250-75
Magnus Barn-Lock	1275-90
Torgils Knutsson (regent)	1290-98
Birger Magnusson	1290-1318
Magnus Eriksson	1319-95
Albrecht of Mecklenburg	1364-89
Margaret (regent)	1389-1412
Engelbrekt	1435-36
Karl Knutsson	1436-40
Christopher	1448-57
Karl Knutsson (king)	1448-57
Christian I	1457-64
Karl Knutsson	1467-70
Sten Sture the Elder (regent)	1470-1503
(Hans)	1497-1501
Svante Sture (regent)	1503-12
Sten Sture the Younger (regent)	1512-20
Christian II	1520-21

(The Vasa Dynasty)

Gustavus (I) Vasa (regent)	1521-23
(king)	1523-60
Erik XIV	1560-68
John III	1568-92
Sigismund	1592-99
Charles IX (regent)	1599-1604
(king)	1604-11
Gustavus (II) Adolphus	1611-32
Christina	1632-54
Charles (X) Gustavus	1654-60
Charles XI	1660-97
Charles XII	1697-1718
Frederick I	1720-51
Adolphus Frederick	1751-71
Gustavus III	1771-92
Gustavus (IV) Adolphus	1792-1809

Russian Rulers

Alexander I	1801-25
Nicholas I	1825-1855
Alexander II	1855-81
Alexander III	1881-1894
Nicholas II	1894-1917

Presidents of the Republic

K.J. Ståhlberg	1919-25
Lauri Kr. Relander	1925-31
P.E. Svinhufvud	1931-37
Kyösti Kallio	1937-40
Risto Ryti	1940-44
C.G.E. Mannerheim	1944-46
J.K. Paasikivi	1946-56
U.K. Kekkonen	1956-81
Mauno Koivisto	1982-

Reindeer

INDEX

Page numbers that appear in boldface type indicate illustrations

125

About the Author

Martin Hintz is a self-employed writer who specializes in travel with an emphasis on the personalities and culture of an area rather than simply destinations. Finland is one of his favorite locales. He considers the Finns—molded by their long, dark winters and tempered by their vibrant, alive summers—as among the most interesting people he has ever met. Not long ago in Helsinki, he purchased a colorful designer dress for his wife Sandy, a set of toy knights for sons Daniel and Stephen, and a row of wooden ducks for daughter Kate. A little toy troll also found its way into his return suitcase. The gifts summed up the best of what the Finns had to offer: the fashionable look of today; a love of history; expertise in handicrafts; and a tongue-in-cheek view of what forces shape the Finnish world. Hintz lives in Milwaukee, Wisconsin. He has a master's degree in journalism from Northwestern University.